the COFFEEHOUSE GOSPEL

SHARING YOUR FAITH IN EVERYDAY CONVERSATION

[RELEVANTBOOKS]
WWW.RELEVANTBOOKS.COM

AUTHOR. MATTHEW PAUL TURNER

Published by Relevant Books
A division of Relevant Media Group, Inc.
www.relevantbooks.com
www.relevantmediagroup.com

© 2004 by Matthew Paul Turner

Design: Relevant Solutions
www.relevant-solutions.com
Design by Joshua Smith
Cover Photography & Assisted Inside Photography: Trey Hill
Relevant Books is a registered trademark of Relevant Media Group, Inc., and is
registered in the U.S. Patent and Trademark Office.

For information or bulk orders:
RELEVANT MEDIA GROUP, INC.
POST OFFICE BOX 951127
LAKE MARY, FL 32795
407-333-7152

Library of Congress Control Number: 2004093615
International Standard Book Number: 0-9746942-8-2

04 05 06 07 9 8 7 6 5 4 3

Printed in the United States of America

The idea for this book was conceived during a conversation with my friend and mentor, Dick Eagan. I would have never written this book without your involvement. Thank you for your continued investment.

This one is for you, Jessica Nicole. Thank you for putting up with my late night writing sessions, my tendency to be A.D.D, and my crazy, wild sense of emotion. You are everything to me. I love you.

Many thanks go out to:

Jesus for Your story; my incredible father and mother for constantly showing me the Gospel of Christ; Melanie, Kelley, and Elisabeth for being the three best sisters in the world; my family-in-law, "The Schims," for allowing your daughter to marry me; my "platoon," Daniel, Lee, Lisa, Julie, Michael, Shawn, Eric, Sean, Lizza, Christa, Jaci, Drew, Rebekah, Stacie, Jeremy, JY, Ryan, Carlo, Cassandra, Dale, Nate, Bebo, and Roshare; Cara, Cameron, Summer, and Kyle and everyone else at Relevant Media Group— You people rock!; Keith and Ron at The Full Armor Group; John Hogen for your friendship and the late night laughs on the "John and Matt" show (Sha Na Na); Stephen Arterburn for your encouragement; Kent County, Maryland, for being a really cool place to grow up; Nick and Kim Serban, Dick and Cheryl Eagan, Brian and Cindy Bowdren for your love and support; The Fish Milwaukee; Julie Johnson and everyone else at Compassion International; Amy for the eggs and bacon at Le Peep; Aaron, Bart and Jessica for the editorial help; Mandy Collinger for your friendship and "savvy" publicity moves; C.S. Lewis for *Mere Christianity*; Mac for the Powerbook G4

»FOREWORD

All of us communicators sure do talk a lot. We use a lot of big words to say the same old stuff. And so often we are just talking and writing to ourselves. We talk to ourselves so much that we get defensive because someone else does not say the same old stuff exactly the way we do. Then along comes someone like Matthew Paul Turner. He is not talking to my generation; he is talking to a new generation and even the generation after that. He has transcended all people-pleasing editorial comments and produced a work about real faith and what it is to live the real life with Christ.

I am so glad you found this book, because in reading it, you may find yourself. You may want to dig deeper into the whys and hows of your own personality and the conflicts it bears that prevent you from taking the Gospel wherever you go.

Let me assure you that while Matthew is clever and funny and one of the most creative men in America, he is the real deal, and we all get to benefit because of it.

I hope you enjoy *The Coffeehouse Gospel* as much as I did and as much as so many enjoyed Matthew's first book, *The Christian Culture Survival Guide*.

Stephen Arterburn
Author, *Every Man's Battle*

>> TABLE OF **CONTENTS**

CHAPTER BEGINNING

» INTRODUCTION

CHAPTER BEGINNING

I'VE WORKED IN A COFFEEHOUSE—AND IT wasn't one of those hole-in-the-wall outfits that serve really bad coffee under poor fluorescent lighting, either. I worked at a real, independent coffeehouse that served the finest coffee made from the finest beans money could buy. We purchased beans from all over the world—cool places like Jamaica, Colombia, Guatemala, and Tanzania. My coffeehouse's lighting was warm and contemporary, and its design was industrial yet welcoming. One couldn't help but want to stay and be

involved in the experience. That was our goal at Jammin'
Java—to be a community gathering place for all.

During my time at Jammin' Java, I experienced
firsthand how the culture and environment of a
coffeehouse makes it very easy to build relationships,
talk about deep topics and completely disagree, yet
remain the closest of friends. Although the topics
of discussion included various views on music,
politics, faith, movies, and current events—and there
were plenty of disagreements—the coffeehouse was
always a place that welcomed differences in opinions.
Everyone—no matter the individual's background and
viewpoints—felt appreciated, or at least, listened to.

The coffeehouse is no longer just small business.
Look at the success of Starbucks. It's one of fastest
growing companies in the world. The famous coffee
conglomerate's goal is not only to be a place that
guarantees the best coffee in town, but to also be a
person's "third" environment, after his or her workplace
and home.

The past ten years have been a revolution of sorts
for the coffeehouse. It's once again become the world's
meeting place in today's modern culture. And it
certainly doesn't surprise me. The equation is pretty
simple. Take a healthy addiction; make the "habit"
environment plush and comfortable. Add a few good
looking, interesting people behind the counter to
serve as your "dealers." What do you get? A magical
community experience that attracts young, old,
wealthy, poor, smart, dumb, the incredibly hip, and
complete losers to come and partake in the rich, warm
environment of a coffeehouse.

Such an environment is a good place for the Gospel of

Christ. The message of Jesus is freeing, unassuming, and provocative. It makes thinkers out of the most shallow of people. The good news needs room to move and an atmosphere that provokes thought, meditation, and open discussion. The message that often remains stifled up inside the haughty walls of church buildings finds new life when displayed in a non-formulaic manner within an open environment where the opinions of all are respected and honored.

The Coffeehouse Gospel isn't about Jesus being shared in the comfy surroundings of a coffeehouse. On the contrary, this book will help you re-discover your call to share your personal story in the everyday.

The art of evangelism is not one to be mastered; it's more lifestyle than duty and more natural process than calculated function of necessity. It's God's resounding request for His followers to participate in His story. Your spiritual, mental, and emotional involvement is key to being an engaged follower of Jesus who naturally and effortlessly shares your faith story. God has called you to participate. Will you?

Here's to your story reflecting God's,
Matthew Paul Turner

HAVE YOU EVER THOUGHT ABOUT WHAT it is you're called to do? When you wake up in the morning, is there one certain passion that monopolizes your thoughts? What drives you? Is it music? Is it your career? Perhaps it's a ministry that busies your mind?

When I was sixteen years old, I thought for sure that God had called me to be the Michael Jackson of Christian music. *Yes, I'm actually serious.* Not to be prideful, but I knew I could sing. I thought I could dance. (My friends now inform me that I have the body rhythm of a large tree that's being swayed to and fro by the wind.) Nevertheless, when I was a teenager, I would stand in front of my mom and dad's large bedroom mirror and practice my dance moves to the catchy pop Jesus music of Michael W. Smith and Amy Grant for several hours a week. I'd spike my hair, put on my coolest Ocean Pacific threads, use an old hairbrush as a microphone, and perform for a pretend crowd of thousands of people. Despite all of that practice, my "Thriller" calling—*thank the good Lord*—never panned out. Upon moving to Nashville to pursue my career in music, I realized—as quirky as it sounds—there were *many* untalented Christians with my Michael Jackson calling. Unfortunately, some are still chasing after that dream.

Of course, I've had several life callings. From the foregone dreams of being a veterinarian, a pharmacologist, and a psychologist to my undying quest to thrill audiences with a non-sexual, Jesus-induced version of the King of Pop's musical savvy, my personal callings have always been a driving force for me throughout my life. When we feel called to do something, we spend our lives practicing it, pursuing it, getting educated for it, and so on. For me, pursuing, thinking, and worrying about my calling was sometimes overwhelming and taxing, but that never stopped me from at least working toward it. The same is true of the call for Christians to share the Gospel of Jesus Christ.

Nearly a year and a half ago, I was leaving a quaint little coffeehouse in East Nashville. As I walked across the parking lot with my cell phone to my ear (I had just broken up with a girlfriend and was feeling rather nauseated at the time), a young fellow about my age approached me. He was casually dressed in jeans and a sweatshirt and carrying a very full black backpack. He started walking alongside of me, and it was obvious by the way he was acting that he was going to ask me for more than just directions.

Clearly, I heard God's voice inside my heart telling me to talk with this stranger. I motioned for the young man to wait a moment while I finished my phone call.

When I got off the phone, he looked at me and shared his "I-just-moved-to-town-from-Ohio-and-have-no-money" sad story before asking me if I had a smoke he could bum. It seemed like an innocent question, yet fear overcame me. *I don't have any cigarettes*, I thought to myself. *And there is no way he is getting into my car.* My proneness to drama kicked in—*what might he have in his backpack?* I had a million thoughts rushing through my brain.

I wholeheartedly decided to ignore God's nudge. I wasn't in the mood to exhaust myself with a needy stranger. I was too invested into the events of the evening. So, instead of striking up a conversation or offering to take him to the nearest gas station and buy him a pack of smokes, I looked at him and said, "Sorry, dude, I can't help you." I went my way, and he went his.

I watched him continue walking through the parking lot, and on up the road. After that, I didn't think much about "weird backpack boy" for the rest of the evening.

That young man came to my mind a few weeks later when I had the pleasure of hearing author Brennan Manning (*The Ragamuffin Gospel, Abba's Child*) speak at a local church here in Nashville. The seventy-year-old, chain-smoking, former Catholic priest, wearing a simple pullover shirt and patchwork dungarees, stood in front of five hundred or more people and talked about love. *Real* love. Manning exhorted the audience to be the hands and feet of Jesus. And in doing so, he said, we have the ability to affirm the life and dreams of a broken individual. It was truly one of the most powerful messages I have ever heard.

I realized, after hearing Manning speak, that I had an opportunity that night, outside the little coffeehouse, to possibly have had an impact on an individual's life. In fact, it was clear that God had sent him my way. And I know what you're thinking: *He simply could have been a kid from Ohio with a seri-*

ous need for nicotine. I realize that, yet he could have been someone I was supposed to know. However, I allowed my fear—as stereotypical and ridiculous as it might have been—to take that opportunity away. How many times have you felt God nudge you, and you ignored it? Sure, it happens, but I often wonder what I missed in the process. What would God have done in my life or the life of the young man if I had simply said, "Yes, I'll obey You"?

No calling on my life is more engaging and at the same time stressful than God's call for me to be His witness. It's engaging, because it's an absolute honor to even be considered to carry such a life-changing message to the masses. Jesus' message of salvation from sin is a challenging, insane, healing message that I am honored to share. Yet it's also a stressful calling, because I often feel inadequate to be a vocal advocate of a holy God's spiritual agenda. My personal sin, insecurities, and fear often keep my ability to speak truth into the lives of others at bay. Though I've certainly witnessed Christians flaunting their treasure of truth flamboyantly, more often than not it's more of a temptation to remain quiet and not say or do anything at all. Usually it's fear and laziness that sends us running. I've been there; I know how hard it is to speak up about Jesus. But all of my many doubts about sharing Jesus with a lost world do not seem to keep Him from asking me to keep doing it.

Sure, God's desire for His followers to bear witness of His love through Christ is indeed an intense request—even mind-boggling at times. It's a request that all of us as Christians should take seriously. Much like a witness taking the stand in a court of law and sharing what he witnessed to be the truth in front of a jury, a judge, and a couple of lawyers, Christians are also called to be witnesses to the power, grace, and mercy we have experienced through a relationship with Christ. Of course, all of us go through times when we fail to really feel the weight and significance of being God's witnesses. Unlike the frivolous dreams we've considered callings in the past (i.e. my calling to be the Michael Jackson of Christian music), God's passion for us to share His story should be a relentless drive that burns in our hearts and minds. But let's face it: Sharing the Gospel with others is usually something that ends up in the backs of our minds and only reveals itself when the opportunity is obvious. Most of us can probably admit that sharing our faith is not on our daily to-do list. But it should be.

I don't believe our blasé attitude reflects our will to witness. Most Christians want to be a part of God's grander picture for their lives—yet we simply fail to engage ourselves in our calling to answer that call.

Most of us *want* be considered His "star" witnesses. We *want* to see God move through our words and

His glory revealed. Heck, we *want* to be Elijah-type defenders of the faith. But all too often, knowing exactly how to connect the *desire* with our *actions* doesn't come easy, and the risks can be ridiculous—sometimes even humiliating. If you've ever stepped out of your comfort zone in an attempt to share your faith and ended up feeling like you're standing buck naked in the middle of a large crowd of complete strangers—you have some idea of what I mean when I say witnessing can be hard and humiliating.

To put it bluntly, it's just plain scary stepping out on the limb of faith and opening up to a stranger about your love for Jesus—especially when you're not sure there's a safety net to catch you if you fall, and you are quite sure the ground below is as hard as concrete. The calling for all of us to share our faith does require a great leap of faith, but I've learned over the years through practice, experience, and watching God move, it's a leap worth taking.

QUESTIONS TO CONSIDER:

1. What is your calling?
2. Do you see God's desire for us to be His witnesses as a part of that calling?
3. What's your attitude toward sharing your faith?

4. Have you had bad experiences witnessing that have left you fearful to answer that call?

JESUS CALLS AT THE MOST INCONVENIENT TIMES

I'm sure if you've been following Jesus for any length of time, you've been subject to Jesus' poor sense of *earthly* timing. Just reading some of the stories in the Bible, it's clear that God has a very different set of rules when it comes to timing. To us, Jesus tends to call on us to make statements on His behalf at the most inopportune moments. He usually knocks on my heart's door when I'm feeling too tired, irritable, and unmotivated to talk Gospel with a stranger. It isn't that I want to avoid sharing truth; I just tend to be lazy—a truth that I don't care to admit sometimes.

However, as Christians, all our lives are lived on-call. God is constantly using His people to fulfill His ultimate earthly destiny—that His glory be revealed around the world through the redemptive power of His Son, Jesus. And He accomplishes this through us, His kids. So no matter how weird and seemingly senseless God's concept of our time schedule is, we're on-call to be His disciples whether or not we like it, desire it, or understand it.

ANDY TOBBS, CONSTRUCTION WORKER

It was a rather warm December afternoon. I had been cooped up inside my home office all morning long, doing rewrites for my first book. I had decided to walk outside for a breath of fresh air. Andy, a thirtysomething construction worker, was out by his truck. Our eyes met in one of those awkward "why are you staring at me?" glances. Being somewhat willing to chat with anyone, I said hello to him.

"Pretty day, isn't it?" I said.

"D--- right. Hard to believe it is December," Andy said in his thick southern drawl.

"Yeah, I was planning on going Christmas shopping, but it's hard to get in the mood when it's 65 degrees outside."

"Yeah, well, I haven't felt much like Christmas shopping this year," said Andy rather bluntly.

"Oh yeah? Why not?" I questioned.

"I'm going through a divorce," Andy said, "And that b---- of mine is trying to take my two kids away from me. She won't stop pestering me with legal s---."

It's always funny to me how some people are so comfortable sharing their life's baggage with a complete stranger. Maybe it's just me, but I find that people in today's society are very open to talking about their struggles, disappointments, and fears. All the while we were talking, Andy was rummaging through his toolbox, looking for a socket wrench.

"I'm sorry to hear about the divorce; divorce sucks. Hey, what's your name?"

"I'm Andy."

"Andy, it's nice to meet you. My name is Matthew. You know, I have a friend who is going through a very similar situation."

"Yeah?"

"Yup. He's having a hard time, too. He's actually been going to a counselor. Have you been to any type of therapy to help you through this?"

"Yeah, my wife dragged me in to see some preacher she knows. After one visit, I had had enough of that s---."

"Hmm, why is that?"

"That man had nothing to teach me. All he said was that we should start going to church ..."

I was pretty sure the pastor had said more than just that, but I didn't want to question Andy.

"You grow up in the church?" I asked, thinking to myself, *Here's my chance.*

"Nah. Did you?" retorted Andy.

"Yeah, I did. Although, I must admit that I've never particularly enjoyed going to *church.* I've always pursued a relationship with God. I couldn't survive without God in my life."

"That's cool," he said, seeming uninterested.

"Well, man, I need to get back to writing.

For what it's worth, I'll keep your situation in my prayers."

"Yeah, I need to get back to work, too. Nice meeting you."

+I ran into Andy one other time. His divorce had been finalized, but was still in a custody battle for his children. I still keep Andy in my prayers.

Even as a child growing up in a conservative white Baptist church, I was always intrigued by the manner in which Jesus called His disciples to follow Him and their willingness to just follow with blind faith. The Bible teaches us that the disciples were simple—extremely ordinary—men who were working as fishermen and tax collectors and doing other remedial jobs. They were all minding their own business when Jesus called to them and simply said, "Follow me." There was no explanation as to why Jesus was calling them and what it was He wanted them to do. His request was blunt, somewhat cocky, and very ambiguous. Yet the disciples followed with an abandon that I find hard to comprehend. Can you imagine what that might have felt like?

Equate the "Jesus calling His disciples" scenario to what you experience on a daily basis. Imagine if Jesus would have chosen to walk on earth in the twenty-first century. One day, not unlike any other day, you're doing your normal routine—busy working at Starbucks, selling stocks and bonds on Wall Street, or taking one of your five college courses. Then right smack in the middle of your day, Jesus comes by and says, "Hey *you*, follow me." He doesn't tell you that He is the chosen one. There's no hint that He's a miracle worker. To you, He just seems like a very passionate person with a somewhat weird desire to have a few followers to rally alongside Himself. Would you go with, no questions asked?

Sure, you might think this exercise is a bit strange—perhaps even silly—but it certainly makes one think. Would you have been one of the first twelve people to leave the comfort of your personal existence and follow Jesus? Truthfully, I probably would have thought Jesus was a crazy fanatic and just ignored Him, and perhaps even laughed at Him—not to mention that my family would have gone ballistic if I called them one day and told them I was going to leave my job as a writer and instead, follow this man who was claiming to be the son of God around the poor places of the world. Yet as strange as this scenario is—isn't it exactly what we're called to do?

Even though more than two thousand years have passed since Jesus called His first disciple to chase after him, Jesus is *still* in the business of calling new disciples to leave everything behind and follow Him. Ironically, a life of pursuing the things of Christ shouldn't be much different today than it was during Jesus' earthly visit. We are His disciples. No, we don't have the tangibility of His hands touching our faces or an audible voice telling us to "fear not," but nevertheless, we're called to follow Him with blind faith.

In other words, if you're a follower of Jesus, you've been called to be His witness. It's a beautiful calling that not only requires your active and ongoing participation, but it also requires braveness, intensity, and complete surrender.

You in? Are you sure?

QUESTIONS TO CONSIDER:

1. Have you ever had a poorly timed Jesus calling? If so, what did you do?

2. What do you learn from the disciples' willingness to leave everything behind and follow Jesus? Do you feel you would have done the same? Do you now?

GO FISH

When Jesus began calling out the names of His disciples, one of the first things He told them was that He would make them "fishermen of people." Despite this unusual calling, twelve men left twelve ordinary jobs and followed Jesus. They left everything in pursuit of a better life following a self-proclaimed God-man.

Call me a cynic, but if I had heard Jesus tell me He was going to make me a "fisher of men," I believe I would have wanted to know a little more information before there would have been any chance of me saying yes. The Bible doesn't imply that the disciples asked such questions. I would have no doubt been the one to ask Jesus for a detailed explanation: *Okay, Jesus, give me the rundown of all the benefits there are of following You and You making me a fisher of men, and I'll give it some consideration.* Jesus gave Peter and crew no such explanation. In fact, it was quite some time before Jesus confided in them and foretold the grave destiny of their calling. We see proof of this in Matthew 10:16-18.

Jesus said, "Look, I am sending you out as sheep among wolves. Be as wary as snakes and harmless as doves. But beware! For you will be handed over to the courts and beaten in the synagogues. And you must stand trial before governors and kings because you are my followers. This will be your opportunity to tell them about me—yes, to witness to the world." (NLT)

Beaten in the synagogues? Again, I would have piped up right about then with a couple more questions: *Jesus, why didn't You tell us we'd be beaten, mocked, and ridiculed for following You and preach-*

ing Your name? Why are you dropping this informa-
tion on us now? But again, the disciples offered no
such questions. By the time Jesus told the disciples
about their somewhat depressing destiny, they had
seen the miracles of Christ. They had watched Jesus
influence thousands by the sound of His voice. It had
been by faith that they first followed, yet by this time,
they had a little tangible understanding to help their
faith along.

Today, when Christians confidently and decidedly
step up to the spiritual plate and make a statement
of their faith in Christ, there will be consequences—
both good and bad. I've had moments of glory-filled
witnessing when people tear up at the sound of my
voice describing the perfect peace I find in a relationship with Christ. But I've also been laughed at, ridiculed, and mocked for my statements of faith. I don't
consider what I have encountered persecution—not
even close—but I do know what it feels like to make
a stand for Jesus only to be knocked down in the end.
Again, it's that "buck naked in the middle of a crowd"
feeling.

No matter the cost, Jesus expects His people to
walk—blindly, if necessary—where He leads them.
He seems to call the simple minded—those of us
who would jump courageously into a life of following
Him and proclaiming His message. He certainly isn't
looking for the weak or the faint of heart. He desires

witnesses who will completely engage themselves in their calling. The first disciples of Jesus may have been ordinary by earthly standards, but their faith to trust and follow Christ was extraordinary. Are you willing to do the extraordinary?

In today's culture, in order for us to be effective witnesses of Christ, there must be a willingness to walk out in faith and accept the challenge of the call God has set before us. Let's face it: The mere thought of sharing our faith openly and freely in today's culture scares some of us. Just like standing buck naked in front of a crowd of strangers, it's frightening just to think about it. It's nerve-wracking. It's difficult. Sharing your faith is scary because we don't know how an individual is going to respond, or how we'll be perceived. We're claiming to have a personal relationship with something unseen. We believe a God-man was conceived by the Holy Spirit, lived a perfect life, and then died on the cross for our sins. We believe He rose again on the third day. That's really extreme. Of course, we're going to have some disheartening feelings toward sharing what we know to be true. Why? Because many in the world today don't comprehend the concept of Jesus. We run the risk of being seen as a fanatic or a lunatic. Don't be surprised by your fear to share the Gospel; it's scary sometimes.

Yet the fear that being God's witnesses brings upon us doesn't negate the fact it's indeed our calling.

How do you currently live out God's calling on you to share your faith? Are you the type of person who only talks about your faith when one of your non-Christian friends asks a question? Perhaps, you're the fearless type who quickly leads the lost down the "Romans Road," only to come across forceful and judgmental. Jesus didn't ask the disciples what type of personality each of them had. He asked them to give Him their all. No matter their differences, Jesus used each one of them in an extravagant manner.

Peter was outspoken and loud. John was thoughtful and loving. Thomas was inquisitive and fearful. Yet God used each of them in a mighty fashion despite their personality flaws. The same is true for us.

God uses all types of personalities to advance His kingdom with their faith stories. So, no matter if you're shy, bold, obnoxious, A.D.D., funny, boring, ugly, or cute, if you're a follower of Jesus, He's called you to share your life story as a statement of His mercy, grace, love, and forgiveness.

QUESTIONS TO CONSIDER:

1. What are your fears in sharing your faith?
2. When Jesus called His disciples to be "fishers of men," what do you think He meant by that?

3. What are your strengths and weaknesses
in sharing your faith?

A WAKE-UP CALL TO ACTION

I remember vividly the first time I realized the significance of being called to be God's witness.

I was twenty-two years old, and I had just graduated from college. Although I had known Christ since
a very early age, evangelism and witnessing were always task-oriented responsibilities that I did because
I had to do them—not because I thought I was called
to do so. And my church's methods for evangelism
were often outrageously rigid and very embarrassing.
I was raised in a church that practiced the method
of going door-to-door throughout a town and asking
people if they knew Jesus. We were about as popular
as the Jehovah's Witnesses or those Mormon missionaries we see from time to time wearing white
short-sleeved shirts, ties, and plastic name tags.
Some folks would hide from us when they saw us
coming. Thinking back, I probably would have, too.

However, despite my uncomfortable history of
using old-fashioned evangelism tactics to witness to
Jesus' impact on my life, that first year out of college,
God gave me a wake-up call to my responsibility to
witness that I will remember for the rest of my life.

I was working at a brand new live music venue

and restaurant in Nashville, Tennessee. I was one of twenty servers who was hired as part of the opening staff. And gosh, I had no clue what I was doing or what I was about to encounter. At times, I look back on this time in my life and wonder if it was for real.

Being a new server, I had to learn quickly that many of the servers I worked with lived by very different life rules than I was accustomed to. Think MTV *Real World* on a never-ending overdose of crack. These people worked long hours. Due to their long hours, many of them were irritable and moody. Most of them had no desire to be working as servers, yet they did it because they had to and were waiting with bated anticipation of something better to come along. Oh, and yes, most of the servers I worked with were all either drug addicts, alcoholics, gothic-prone God haters, atheists, or gay—and a couple of them were all of the above. It was a rather eclectic group of people to say the least.

Having been raised as a conservative Baptist in Small Town, U.S.A., with very little experience working around professional sinners (and when I say professional, I mean sinners who were really passionate and quite talented at their sins), my ability to be a God witness was thoroughly tested. I didn't feel necessarily afraid to witness, just unprepared. And it wasn't that I thought I was better than those I worked around. But for the first time in my life, I was surrounded by people whose daily passions consisted of talking about their enjoyment of anal sex, taking hits of heroin and other hard-core narcotics, and doing their best job at proving my God didn't exist. At first, I was angry and scared. Then I was overcome with guilty heaviness. But mostly, I was convinced that I was *way* out of my league.

Of course, knowing that it was my spiritual duty to inform the sinners that they were in fact, umm, sinners, I made sure my fellow colleagues knew where I stood on matters of faith, God, and their godless actions. That went over like a lead balloon. I'd had Jesus conversations with most of them. I practiced every evangelical rule I had ever been taught growing up in church. I asked them questions like this: Do you know that you're a sinner in need of God's forgiveness? Did you know that God hates what you're doing? Do you even care what God thinks? After pounding them with my million and one questions, I would transition into a "by the way, did you know that Jesus loved you enough to die for your sins on the cross? In fact, He even loves you."

I never got any of them to pray the sinner's prayer—heck, most of them wouldn't stop talking about the fact that they really loved their sin long enough to even hear what I had to say. So instead of being intrigued by my conversations about God, they used my lack of biblical knowledge, my stupid spiritual comebacks, and my Christian innocence against me. Needless to say, I felt defeated, deflated, and disengaged. I remedied my situation by shutting up and avoiding spiritual conversations with them altogether. It worked, too. Instead of trying to preach my way through every conversation, I would just listen, and then pray for God to open up opportunities for me to share my faith.

One day, two months into my new position, one of the other servers (it was one of the gay guys who had a fetish for men who wore women's underwear. I'm not kidding you) and I were folding napkins and rolling silverware. We started talking about life—actually, we talked about *my* life. He began asking me questions. So, I shared with him my personal story. It wasn't a perfect rendition of the four spiritual laws by Rick Warren, but it wasn't the Three Little Pigs, either. I just started sharing with him my everyday struggles with work, dating, and family and how I saw God working in my life on an everyday basis. Surprisingly, my colleague listened. He actually *really* listened. I walked away from that conversation simply thanking God that He had opened up the opportunity for me to talk about Him.

Sadly, and perhaps surprisingly to you, I had never realized until then that sharing my faith was so much more than just saying the words, "I believe Jesus died for your sins and that is how you get to go to heaven."

It's so much more than that. God hasn't made our responsibility in evangelism difficult. However, I believe He does expect us to make an effort to truly know and understand the Gospel of Jesus Christ and to work at knowing how to relate this truth to others. It isn't brain surgery, but how many of us take the time to assess our approach to being God's witness? How many of us actively pursue bettering ourselves in sharing God's story? Perhaps I'm in the minority, but until that day, I hadn't.

My chat with that server made me realize that sharing my faith was not a hard-core "do-it-or-you-lose" task. Witnessing should feel as natural as breathing. It should be seamless and effortless. Although I believe it's a calling from God to share my faith in the everyday, I also believe He's given all of us a personal story to share—stories that simply show non-Christians many different pictures of the grace of Christ. These life stories are real circumstances that can simply give an individual who is lost a different perspective on eternal truths, passions, and life.

The journey of our calling begins with a wake-up call—a call that reminds us first that our responsibility to be Christ's witnesses to others isn't a part-time job—it's everyday, twenty-four hours a day. But secondly, our stories, every minor detail—good and bad—are key to letting people see what it is Christ is in the business of doing in the lives of people.

QUESTIONS TO CONSIDER:

1. Have you had your own wake-up call? What did it feel like for you the first time you realized your responsibility to share your faith?

2. Have you ever been in a situation where you're trying to share your faith, but instead of witnessing God's love, you end up saying something really dumb? (Be honest; it happens to the best of us.)

COFFEEHOUSE GOSPEL TRUTH #1:

   YOU WILL NO DOUBT EXPERIENCE
wake-up calls throughout your life. God makes us
sharper through wake-up calls. He uses them to
make our "light" shine brighter and our "salt" more
seasoned. Wake-up calls are His way of reminding
us that we're a part of a greater plan. It's a plan He
designed, and while at times, His plans may seem

strange or complicated to you, that's how God works. His ways are not our ways.

During the summer of 2000, I ventured to Europe on a mission trip with my church, Vienna Presbyterian, in Vienna, Virginia. We teamed up with an organization called New Hope International to go to Romania. There were seventeen Americans on the trip, and it was our responsibility to run a youth camp for Romanian teenagers in the mountains just west of the city of Kluj-Napoca. I had never been on a trip outside of the United States, except for one trip to the Canadian side of Niagara Falls. It was an amazingly eye-opening trip during which I learned a great deal about God's call to go into all the world and preach the Gospel.

While in Romania, tucked away in the Transylvanian mountains, I met a sixteen-year-old young man named Bennie. He was a shy, quiet kid from one of the poorest areas of Romania. I don't think Bennie showered once that whole week, and it showed. (He stunk to high heavens. If I had been a meaner person, I would have given him my stick of deodorant, but I abstained.) And while many of the teenagers spoke semi-fluent English, Bennie could only speak in his native tongue—and according to the other Romanians, he could barely do that. I felt sorry for the kid and instantly, despite my keen sense of smell, took a liking to him. And despite Bennie's and my inability to *verbally* communicate, we became the best of friends that week through smiles, nods, eye contact, and a common interest in volleyball.

On the last evening of our time at the camp, during the praise and worship service, Bennie and I were sitting next to each other. We both looked rather ridiculous. Our bodies were sunburned, our muscles were tired, and our voices were strained from the week's activities. All of us in the group were singing Rich Mullins' song "Awesome God" in Romanian. Well, I was attempting to sing it, but the enunciation of the words proved difficult for me. So I just hummed along.

Suddenly, with my eyes closed, singing worship music in a foreign language, I felt Bennie reach over and grab my hand, holding it tightly in his grip. *Okay, God. What is Bennie doing?* My first response was this feeling of discomfort that formed in my gut. My homophobic Baptist roots were still very much intact, so the idea of a guy holding my hand in public was simply not kosher to say the least. I thought about pulling away before one of the other leaders accused me with some kind of molestation charge. But God spoke. And He spoke loud. He said, *"Matthew, you're not in America anymore, and you're not playing by your rules. You're playing by My rules. Trust Me on this one."*

At that moment of obedience, miraculously, I felt

an unexpected peace come over me. It was somewhat surreal. Bennie and I held hands, cried, hugged, and worshiped throughout the rest of the service. We were both moved by God's presence.

In the midst of all of this, Jesus taught me something about sharing my faith through this rather uncomfortable experience. I learned that my ability to share His love was sometimes crippled by my own selfish fear—a fear that originated from the stereotypes I had developed as a child. No, I don't plan on making it a habit of going around and holding hands with guys during praise and worship services. But one thing I did learn from Bennie is that sometimes sharing my faith requires me to come out of my comfort zone. Sometimes sharing my faith requires me to de-Americanize myself—to put myself completely and blindly in the hands of God and allow Him to use me.

So often as Christians, we let our comfort zones define and mold our ability to open up and experience God fully using us. We all do it. Our comfort zones are built by us, managed by us, and developed by us to protect *us*. However, the man and woman who burn with a desire to be candid in their faith stories doesn't let a comfort zone come between them and a God experience. Daniel went bravely before the king to speak God's message. Esther risked her life to save her people. David walked out in front of a massive giant with no armor and a slingshot. All of these men and women left their comfort zones to pursue their higher callings.

How many times have you allowed your comfort zone to dictate your ability to share Christ? My time in Romania taught me a great deal, but my most important lesson while there was learning to take "me" out of the spiritual equation of witnessing. If I make a habit of calculating my fears, my insecurities, and my stereotypes into God's overall expectation of me to tell His story, I'm going to miss His will every time. You will, too. If we want to effectively share our faith, we must take the "me" out of the overall God equation.

One of the most compelling ways to express your faith in the everyday is through the selfless portrayal of God's story in you. We have to break down the barriers that have been built up in our hearts since our childhood. Perhaps you're still holding on to non-redemptive thoughts about a particular race, business affiliation, political party, sexual preference, or other stereotypes we've all been guilty of in the past. But a person sharing their faith freely tries to avoid being manipulated by the Christian and secular worlds' ideas of safety and comfort. Just like the disciples abandoned all they knew to be home, we must abandon fears, misconceptions, and intolerance to be completely used by Christ.

1. What stereotypes have you developed over the years? Do they keep you from ministering freely?

2. What is your definition of selflessness?

JESUS SPEAKS OF SELFLESSNESS

If we as Christians desire to abandon the strongholds that keep us from sharing the Gospel, we must investigate our hearts on a daily basis. Continuous reflection and renewal of the heart is so important to our influence as God witnesses. In Jesus' Sermon on the Mount in Matthew 5 through 7, Christ passionately described His heart's desires for His children. He opened up to His followers about what it means to have a mind set on kingdom thoughts. And not surprisingly, Jesus turned His own thoughts and words toward the treatment of others and the condition of the heart. The first few verses of Matthew 5 are considered some of the most precious words ever spoken by Christ. These are the Beatitudes:

Jesus said,
"God blesses those who realize their need for him, for the Kingdom of Heaven is given to them.

God blesses those who mourn, for they will be comforted.

God blesses those who are gentle and lowly, for the whole earth will belong to them.

God blesses those who are hungry and thirsty for justice, for they will receive it in full.

God blesses those who are merciful, for they will be shown mercy.

God blesses those whose hearts are pure, for they will see God.

God blesses those who work for peace, for they will be called the children of God.

God blesses those who are persecuted because they live for God, for the Kingdom of Heaven is theirs.

God blesses you when you are mocked and per-secuted and lied about because you are my followers.

Be happy about it! Be very glad! For a great reward awaits you in heaven. And remember, the ancient prophets were persecuted, too."
(NLT)

These verses are certainly difficult for some of us to truly comprehend. Some people have called the Beatitudes God's "to-do list." Do we *really* believe that God blesses those who have pure hearts or those who are persecuted for speaking truth or those who work for peace? Do we *really* believe this? I think sometimes we struggle to understand what is means to be pure, peaceful, meek, and hungry and thirsty.

I believe Christ's "heart" message in these ten verses can be summed up with one word: selflessness. I highly recommend you re-read Jesus' entire Sermon on the Mount (Matthew 5-7). Throughout this sermon, Christ made emphatically clear His intent to focus on the selfish condition of man's heart. Almost as soon as His ministry began, Jesus used His words to chip away at man's hardened and selfish hearts. Before Christ could send out His followers as representations of Him, He knew there was "heart" work to be done. He knew that in order for people to truly see Himself through humanity, humanity needed to make changes to their current lifestyle.

The same is true today. God needs followers who evaluate their hearts on a continuous basis, searching for selfishness, impurities, and pride.

Jesus wants His followers to not only comprehend the kingdom, but to also live out His kingdom in everyday life. Jesus' kingdom is a part of His story. Jesus desires His story to become a part of His followers' stories. And usually, that begins with our hearts.

An individual with a heart that seeks to create peace, hungers and thirsts for justice, and naturally thinks of others will gravitate toward talking about his or her faith in the everyday. Why? Because that individual realizes that it's not about him or her. That individual realizes this world is temporary, meaningless, and lost, but God's kingdom is not. That kind of person realizes that when Jesus said, "The first shall be last in the kingdom of heaven," He meant it. It wasn't lip service. An individual who longs to be selfless will actively look for opportunities to be last. He will walk into daily situations and realize that there's a greater purpose at work—God's purpose. And he will want to pursue that purpose with all of his heart, soul, and mind. *That* kind of individual will be compelled to pursue a lost world for Christ. He will be led to share his personal God story freely, honestly, and often.

CONVERSATION #2: APRIL 2004:
TODD BISHOP, COLLEGE SENIOR

I recently visited a large university in the Midwest. While there, one of my close friends wanted me to meet her friend Todd. I willingly obliged. We met at this Swedish bar on a side street, just off the college's main drag. I knew very little about the individual I was meeting. What I did know was this: He was gay, democrat, and very intelligent.

We introduced ourselves. He was shorter than I expected. I was probably balder than he expected. Yet despite our preconceived notions, we hit it off quickly over a few laughs.

He ordered a glass of red wine. I ordered a cranberry juice, which came to the table a little too watered down for my liking. And over a couple of drinks, we began talking about life.

"Todd, I've heard a little bit about you, but I want you to tell me more about your personal story. What makes you tick?" I asked. Todd told me he was the only child of two very loving parents. He exited the closet at age nineteen. He hates the gay sub-culture. He would like to go into politics someday. He's a caring person, generally thinking of the thoughts and hearts of others. That's his story in a nutshell.

Without pursuing it, our conversation naturally turned to the eternal.

"You know what, Matthew, I believe there is a God," Todd said convincingly.

"Do you pursue a relationship with God?"

I asked.

"What do you mean?" asked Todd.

"I mean, do you talk to Him? Do you attend a church or another place where you can worship Him? Do you work at knowing who God is in your life?"

"I actually have done that in the past, and to be honest, I'm not sure why I don't anymore. Sometimes it's weird knowing you're gay, yet desiring to have a relationship with a God who everyone tells me hates my lifestyle."

"Well, Todd, I believe no matter who we are or what we're doing, I believe Jesus loves us with all of His heart. I do think He sometimes is disgusted with all of our actions, but at the core of who Jesus is, there's a boundless, unexplainable love I find addicting."

"I know that. And to be completely honest, I'm not your ordinary gay man—you know, the guy who sleeps around with every other guy he can, Matthew. I *do* pray. And I sometimes meditate."

"Todd, I just want you know this: God has given you a bizarre amount of talent. You're a very smart, intelligent individual. And I believe with all my heart that if you'll seek Jesus, He'll reveal Himself to you. His Word promises that."

"Okay. I really appreciate that. And I will do my best."

"God has plans for you, but you will not know those plans without pursuing the relationship He's pursuing in you."

+Todd Bishop has graduated from college. He's pursuing the insane world of politics. We speak over the phone on occasion.

The quest to be selfless is often a lonely pursuit in today's modern, sophisticated, and very selfish culture. Chock full of success-driven individuals only interested in looking out for number one, today's culture is filled with people consumed with careers, image, money, and self-fulfillment. Instead of focusing on the needs of others, we hone in on our own needs for financial comfort, sex, and acceptance, just to name a few. Instead of looking to the needs of others, we invest in ourselves. If we want to be followers of Jesus who talk effortlessly about our faith, we must dispose of our selfishness. And that's not easy to do.

Many of us have let ourselves become programmed by the culture's message of self-investing. We have let ourselves become people who are only motivated by self-advancement and self-glory. We have a mindset of, "How can I help 'me' today?" We're all guilty of this at one time or another. I certainly struggle with naturally thinking of others. Our society works that way, and it's hard not to get sucked into the madness of me, me, *me*.

You can't watch one episode of MTV's *Cribs* without being bombarded with the materialism for which wealthy Americans strive. So many of my friends watch *Cribs* in complete lust for the lush commodities that wealth and celebrity bring in today's society. The same is true watching Donald Trump's *The Apprentice*. Although wildly entertaining, this show depicts sixteen intelligent, hard working individuals who seemingly will employ whatever means necessary to be perceived as successful, business savvy, and powerful. We will long remember the actions of Omarosa who lied and manipulated her way throughout the experience. God's ways don't relate or line up to those of *Cribs* and *The Apprentice*. God's ways are pure and *selfless* and do not succumb to the faltering of "me" investing.

As Christians, God's call on our lives flies in the face of what the world deems cool, successful, and pleasurable. Answering God's call on your life begins with a desire for *selfless* investing and constant renewal of your mind.

Despite what you may think to be true or what you've heard, even inside the bubble of Christian culture, selfish behavior is breeding out of control.

Our selfishness does not keep us from witnessing and sharing our faith; it just eats away at our ability to do it with integrity and grace. How many times have you been subject to the witnessing tactics of an individual who seems to be in ministry for the fame? It's important that our hearts for ministry be motivated by only what is pure and honest.

Sadly, selfish and indulgent Christians get plastered all over the newspapers and TV, are mocked in movies, and have huge "ministry-driven" websites all over the Internet. We've read about sexually promiscuous priests who, for years, have lived selfishly—investing their sexual desires onto the lives of innocent children—behind closed doors. We listen to heads of ministries and televangelists beg us for more money, only to find out years later they have been driving BMWs and Hummers and flying to personal engagements on their very own private jets. Even in some of our churches, the pastors are more interested in being local celebrities and building large, powerful, and influential churches, rather than being interested in being humble, poor, and the last in line.

With this kind of media attention everywhere, many would-be followers of Christ see our selfishness, and instead of turning their hearts toward Christ, their stomachs turn in disgust. If today's Christians want to have any kind of impact on our cities or communities, we must pursue selflessness with fervor in our everyday actions. We must go about business, ministry, school, and living with the utmost integrity and selfless behavior.

Christians don't need to be perfect, just consistent in their pursuit of selflessness.

Of course, I don't want to mislead you. We can try for the rest of our lives, and we'd never be *completely* selfless. Our sinful natures make it almost impossible to *not* have moments where we want what is best for us—where we pursue what comes easy and comfortable. However, we often fail to realize that our selfish actions have ramifications. We miss opportunities to share God's story, because our lives are lived for self and not for others.

In my personal journey, I have learned that selfless behavior takes practice. You have to actively work at being selfless. It's a mindset you must dive into on a daily basis. And it's not a mindset obtained overnight. It's a gradual change. It's not easy, but if you start making selfless choices in the small areas of your life, you'll begin to learn the value of selflessness. Consider this short list of ideas:

Gentlemen, let the ladies and guys walk through the door first—while you're holding it.

If you're used to shouting "shot gun" before a group of you and your friends jump into a car—try sitting in the back seat for once.

When you walk into a public setting, notice the needs of others. Old ladies, mothers with children, individuals with special needs—there's always someone in need that may need your help.

Give the homeless guy a dollar. Who cares if you know for sure that he is going to buy cigarettes with it? Remember, this exercise is not about what you think.

I have found that if you make an effort to practice selflessness in the small things, you'll discover that your selfless behavior will spill over into the grander details of your life.

QUESTIONS TO CONSIDER:

1. Do you consider yourself to be selfless?
2. What do you learn about God's desire for His children in the Beatitudes?
3. How can you relate what you learned to sharing your faith in everyday conversation?

YOUR SELFLESS STATEMENT

Two of my favorite historical figures are William and Catherine Booth, the founders of the Salvation

Army. Within the confines of their relatively small and humble life together, God used their pursuit of selflessness to give birth to the largest relief organization in the world. However, it didn't begin as a world relief outfit. It's beginnings were humble, serving a small community outside of London.

In 1865, the Booths, two poor evangelists from London's east side, were led to establish a mission in their poverty stricken community. Their new mission focused on "reaching for the worst" of society. The couple's goal was to fulfill not only the physical and emotional needs of the poor, but their spiritual needs as well. William and Catherine never for an instant forgot how these separate needs interrelated to each other. In addition to the many exhausting hours the Booths invested, hundreds of other Christians volunteered their time, which allowed the mission to grow. In addition to sharing the message of Jesus with their patrons, the Booths also provided shelter for the homeless, food for the hungry, and alcohol rehabilitation for the addicted. It was a hands-on ministry that filled the needs of others.

The Booth's "salt and light" indeed influenced the poor community of East London, but even more powerful, their selfless acts of kindness helped launch the largest organized ministry in the world.

It is this kind of selflessness that Jesus speaks about in His Sermon on the Mount. It's this kind of behavior that changes the world. Why do you think the two verses following the Beatitudes are the "city on a hill" verse and the "salt and light" verse? (See Matthew 5:13 and 14.) I don't believe that was an accident. Jesus is saying, if you long to share your faith in the everyday, pursue a life of meekness, righteousness, and purity of heart. Jesus knows the pure shine and the righteous season.

When I was working for Jammin' Java, that faith-based coffeehouse in Northern Virginia, a lady by the name of Ms. Carolyn would come in every week, order her cup of coffee, and pick up the day-old pastries she would give to the needy. So many times she would grace us with her story of how our stale goodies opened up an opportunity for her to share the God story with one of the recipients. She would often tear up with joy as she beautifully detailed the needs of an individual in our community of Vienna. It didn't matter who it was. Ms. Carolyn helped any-one. Her goal was simply to show the love of Jesus to people. Through her simple selfless acts of gathering bread, Ms. Carolyn influenced people in need of knowing God. Unlike the Booths' ministry, I'm pretty sure Ms. Carolyn's ministry is probably not bound for worldwide notoriety, but that didn't matter. Her story was selflessly lived out through actions and her words of affirmation—and celebrity and wealth was not her goal.

However, an individual working toward selflessness is not limited to feeding the homeless. Selfless behavior is also learning the art of walking into any situation with your eyes and ears open to what surrounds you. Selflessness is seeing a normal trip to Starbucks not merely as a place to grab a quick cup of good coffee, but realizing it's also a chance for you to meet someone who may need to be affirmed with the words of Christ. You may meet someone who is new to the journey of faith, and God has chosen you as one of the stops. A selfless mind is constantly thinking about other people and their place in the kingdom. A selfless mindset goes into every situation thinking about the eternal lives of others and not the temporal life of one's self.

Your community needs you to be selfless. If we begin to follow Jesus' example of humility, we will see doors to be a witness of His grace open wide over and over again.

(Forget about everything you've ever been taught about what it means to be a missionary—now, turn the page.)

IF YOU'RE NEW TO THE THRILL OF
spreading evangelical truth, I must warn you, there
are obstacles to being a daily witness of Christ's love.
Don't get me wrong, there aren't any obstacles you
can't overcome, but it may take some strength, hard
work, and determination on your part.

When it comes to sharing your story in today's culture, Christians everywhere are battling the culture,
and at the same time, attempting also to endure the

smelly religious droppings the fundamentalist Christians leave behind. No matter where you live or how old you might be, you're going to come into contact with weird and wild cultural differences as well as ridiculous people of faith.

However, these obstacles should never keep us from engaging a lost world with truth. Don't laugh; I've certainly had moments where the presence of the evangelical elite has sent me running into spiritual hiding. But I've learned that in everything worth doing, there are obstacles. We still have a responsibility to bear witness to the things Christ has done in our lives whenever we are called to do so. Our journey continues onward when we learn the art of the most humbling spiritual position—the missionary position. It's a position that at times isn't fun and, certainly at times, not easy to get into, but God uses us here.

For me, it came as a newsflash—to realize that we as Christians have all been called to live the life of a missionary.

But to be honest, I, personally, have always struggled with what it truly means for me to be a missionary. My childhood gave me a very limited understanding of what a missionary's job is. I was always taught that being a missionary required leaving your community and venturing to a foreign land to live with people who do not have running water. During this time, you spend your days preaching to people who can't understand you and trying to learn their language.

Perhaps this might come across a little pious and presumptuous, but really, how many of us have a desire or the urge to become a missionary in Cambodia? I don't. It would take a burning bush type sign for me to even begin to consider the concept. I have a great amount of respect and gratitude for those who do answer the call to leave everything behind and take the Gospel of Christ to an unfamiliar territory and culture. But I certainly don't believe we all need to trek halfway around the world and live among indigenous people to be considered missionaries. All of God's followers are missionaries.

For some of us, our definition of missionary has for far too long been limited to the likes of David Livingston and Jim Elliot (if you don't know these two names, Google them. Their lives and ministries will inspire you). I've learned over the years that if you know Jesus, then you should no doubt consider yourself a missionary. Your home, church, community, workplace, campus, or grocery store is your mission field.

As Christians, we are blessed enough to be holding truth in our very hands. I think in some cases—heck, in many cases—we take this for granted. Many of us hold on to God's truth like it's our own personal little treasure.

But the first step to launching into a life of everyday faith conversations is knowing that what you hold is the truth and then realizing your responsibility to share it with others. Being a missionary is most definitely hard work. However, it's also our calling.

I've spoken countless times to men and women who have chosen or have been called to places all over the world to work as full-time missionaries. No matter whom it was I spoke with or where the individual was going, there always seemed to be an uncanny familiarity in the conviction and calling these men and women had on their lives.

The hearts of missionaries are open and gracious. They're determined people, full of passion for the message and selfless desire to go anywhere God leads them. We all need this kind of heart attitude.

A man named Geoffrey Stuart came to my church one Sunday morning several years ago. Stuart was a rather unattractive African-American man, standing about five-foot-seven. He was very round. He wasn't necessarily a great articulator or theologian, but he seemed to have a large heart for people and the Gospel message. Stuart was simply a man with a heart to serve. He was from Montgomery, Alabama, but felt God calling him to the inner city streets of Philadelphia to reach the city's drug addicts, prostitutes, and homeless people. I had lunch with him after the church service and talked with him for an hour about his soul's passion for ministry.

"Hearing God's voice or feeling Him nudge you in a particular direction is like this burning sensation in your gut—at least it is for me," he told me. "My call from God to serve was relentless and also disturbing. I *had* to obey. My heart's craving has always been to serve Jesus and serve Him freely. I try never to question the Holy Spirit's voice; I just respond accordingly."

That conversation with Stuart was so encouraging for me in my own personal quest to be a witness. He shared with me over Subway sandwiches that he thought *hearing* and *listening* to the Holy Spirit was key to being able to freely share the Gospel. I began questioning my own heart: Do I have a heart that desires to listen to the voice of the Holy Spirit? When I do hear His voice, do I respond? Do I ignore God's nudge for me to go into the dark places and be a light?

Stuart came back to speak in front of my church once again two years later. But this time he didn't share what he believed; all he did was tell the stories that he had encountered every day for those last two years while on the streets of Philly. He talked to us about "Helen" who came to know Jesus in a bar one night after Stuart went to see her and her band play a couple times. She was a recovering drug addict, but now God had given her a place in church ministry. He shared his humorous meeting with a gang member who began painting his street with messages about Christ instead of "marking" the gang's territory. I sat there in my pew blown away that God could use such a simple individual to reach such outrageous people. *I'm a simple individual,* I thought, *God could use me, too.*

Stuart's story had grown; his recent encounters with the needy folks from Philly had strengthened his ability to be a witness for Christ's love. Why? Because he watched God move in his life. He heard God tell him to go to Philly. He believed wholeheartedly that God would meet him there. Stuart was willing to see his life like that of a missionary, and he *listened* to God's call.

CONVERSATION #3
INTERVIEW WITH DAN AND GINNY BRYANT, MISSIONARIES IN AFRICA

Dan and Ginny Bryant are church planters and Bible translators in East Africa. I met Dan about three years ago when he visited my church in Maryland. When Dan spoke in front of my church, I was moved by his selflessness. No matter how hard the journey before him seemed, he knew the depth of his calling or "investment" and pursued it wholeheartedly.

Recently, I was able to connect with Dan and talk to him about his initial missionary calling, the risk of investment, and his determination *not* to wrestle with God.

MT: When did God start tugging at your heart to invest the rest of your life into missionary work?

DB: For me, the biggest factor was my parents' influence (they are missionaries in France, and I grew up there). I remember when I was in seventh grade, we talked in school about future careers, and I wrote down "missionary." Part of the process was attending a high school in France and being one of four Christians (that I knew of at least) in a school of two thousand. I realized quickly that there was a big need out there for someone to share the Gospel. It seemed like the best life investment I could think of. The only time that desire wavered is for a two- to three-year period in high school/college when I was not following the Lord. But God brought me back to Himself and "re-motivated" me when I attended a "Perspectives" mission course at my church.

MT: What did God's calling feel like to you? Was it more like a whisper, or did it hit you like a ton of bricks?

DB: For me, missions was more of a "tug,"

something that I wanted to do, and I was psyched to find out that missionaries were still needed to reach isolated people groups (tribes) with the Gospel. So for the most part, missions were always something that I wanted to head toward; if anything, I've wondered about my motivation—was I just doing this because my parents did it, or for the excitement? I also for a time had a bit of an arrogant attitude, thinking it was the most "spiritual" thing to do (I realize now that's not the case).

MT: Were others supportive?

DB: Yes, others were generally very supportive. We have been very blessed in that area.

MT: When Jesus initially presented you with this plan for your life, were there any wrestling matches with Him?

DB: There weren't really any wrestling matches, though there were some big hurdles in my mind—like raising support. I hate the thought of wrestling with God. But even still, He has more than provided for our needs.

MT: Have you seen any "return" on your investment thus far?

DB: Not really. Missionary work is hard in that sometimes it takes years to see a "return."

MT: What have been the scariest moments in your obedience to Jesus?

DB: The scariest time was raising support, especially when we started missionary training with no source of income and only had a summer to visit churches. But perhaps the hardest thing for us was leaving our families; it was much more difficult than I expected. Certainly seeing the long-term purpose for our lives made it a little easier to leave. Leaving really did show us the "cost" of our investment.

MT: How do you and Ginny work together as a team?

DB: Ginny and I are very different in a lot of ways. She sees the big picture. I tend to focus on details. She's a good planner, creative, and a very good communicator. I tend to be more consistent and perhaps more disciplined. So God knew what He was doing in putting us together. We encourage each other by listening and being open with each other. Although, we've certainly had to work on that at times.

MT: Have there been any hard fights with Satan?

DB: The area where he seems to attack the most is discouragement between Ginny and me. We tend to struggle the most with stress during moving times (we've had to move seven times in the last five years). We need to remember to accept each other just like God has accepted us in Christ. Reminding ourselves of this truth has helped a lot. And in terms of discouragement or other stresses, when one of us is struggling, we pray about it together.

MT: Has Jesus changed you at all? Stripped you? Broken you? Lifted you up?

DB: He's increased our faith. During the last several years of being seen as "missionaries," though we may be treated by others as "professional Christians," we are just as much in need of God's grace (if not more so) than others.

MT: Has anything changed about what you "need"—*really* need? How has Jesus helped you deal with not having luxuries and such?

DB: At times, it's been difficult not having a house of our own, or even a permanent place to live. Ginny actually gave a talk at a ladies' retreat on what our real needs are. Our "real" needs are few, aside from knowing Jesus. It's hard to spend much time worrying about the luxuries we don't have, since every time we walk inside the walls of the apartment building where we live, we are struck by how much better off we are than other people here. We don't always have running water or electricity—but at least we have the possibility of filtering the water, and we have appliances and other gadgets to use when there is power.

MT: Is all of this worth it?

DB: It might be better to say that "He is worthy" as we heard someone share recently. In some ways, aside from that principle, the sufferings that some have gone through make it seem like "it's not worth it." However, every investment we have made, God has taught us something new about Himself and about who He wants us to be. If I had to do it all over again, I wouldn't change a thing.

IT BEGINS ON THE INSIDE

Missionary-minded individuals all seem to have the commonality of listening, hearing, and obeying the voice of God. Becoming a man or woman of effortless witness requires a keen ear. It's a holy mindset of sorts. It's waking up in the morning with an overwhelming sense of calling on your life to be a witness of Christ's love and redemption. It's hearing God's voice, but it doesn't conclude with simply hearing—a missionary responds actively to the voice of God.

Hearing God isn't brain surgery, and there really isn't a special art to it. Too many of us have been trained by the Church to think otherwise. God is not in the business of playing games with us. If He wants us to hear Him, He'll make the message as loud and as clear as it needs to be. The Bible is full of people who were surprised by the measures God was willing to take in order for His people to hear His voice. Moses saw the burning bush. David got an earful from the prophet Nathan. Balaam's donkey spoke. The Israelites saw the Red Sea part. The list of biblical examples is endless. If you're open to His voice, God will speak to you all day long. Ask Him to. I often wake up in the morning and ask God, "What do You want me to do today? If there's a conversation You want to have, tell me. I want to follow You, but I need You to make Yourself be known." *God always makes Himself known.*

I've learned you don't have to be Billy Graham or Rick Warren to be a person intently hearing God. I believe God is speaking to His children every day. He's speaking to me right now as I write this book. How do I know? Because I know I am totally incapable of doing anything remotely good without His guidance and wisdom. When it comes to being a witness to the things of God, the same is true for all of us. We cannot be an effective witness without the guidance and wisdom of God.

The Christian's passion to be a missionary begins with hearing God; however, it hardly concludes with hearing. I *heard* God speak to me that evening outside the coffeehouse when He asked to me talk with that stranger, but I did not listen.

We are all guilty of sometimes being fearful, lazy, or

disengaged when it comes to listening to God's voice, especially if He's asking us to take the time to get to know new people. Sometimes the idea is overwhelming, but sometimes it comes as natural as breathing.

There will be times when you hear God's voice loud and clear, telling you to do something. You'll do it, and never really know why God asked you to do it.

As cliché as it might seem, Starbucks is one of my favorite places to strike up conversations with random strangers. (Why do you think this book is called *The Coffeehouse Gospel?*) I've met some of the most interesting people while sitting, reading, writing, and drinking at "Bucks." One morning, I was at sitting in one of the comfy chairs (gosh, I love their chairs), writing this book. While sitting there, a young woman came and sat down in the chair next to me, obviously still waiting for her latte to be made. As soon as she sat down, God said speak to her. I went through my normal negotiating time with God.

Do I have to? I'm really quite busy writing this book, and you know how A.D.D. I am. It will take me forever to get back into concentrating on writing if I begin a conversation now.

I'm notorious for negotiating with God. He patiently hears me out, but usually keeps speaking until I respond with action. I hate that.

God wasn't going to let me out of this one. So I began looking for the right opportunity to say hello to the stranger to my left.

Talking to people has never really been my problem; I talk to people in elevators, airplanes, movie theaters—I'll pretty much talk to anyone at any particular time. My biggest problem is that I tend to just be a little lazy. So, being somewhat the outspoken type—my friends often consider my approach to strangers a little obnoxious—I just looked at her and said a loud and friendly, "Hello."

Before I knew it, I was completely engaged in hearing this woman's life story.

She was a Vanderbilt University graduate student, studying to be a perfusionist. Looking at her with an intuitive grin, she explained to me that a perfusionist is the professional who operates the heart-lung machine during surgeries. She said the hardest part of her job was the constant need to be on call. *For some reason, I highly doubted that was the hardest part of her job.* At any moment of any day, she could be called into perform her duty, and ultimately save a life. After hearing her rather extensive job position, I embarrassingly told her that I was a writer and a speaker. Her response? "Oh, really, that's nice."

After a few minutes spent listening to a detailed explanation that included lots of "blood talk"—which I'm not keen on—I leaned in, shook her hand, and said, "Hello, by the way, my name is Matthew."

"I'm Carolyn," she said, looking at her watch and wondering why the heck her coffee was taking so long.

"Do you live close by?" I asked.

"Yeah, my girlfriend and I live over in the apartments across the street," Carolyn said simply.

Did she just say girlfriend? Instantly, upon hearing the word "girlfriend" coming out of a woman's mouth, my fanatical "Christian" ears perked up, and a rather lengthy dialogue began brewing inside my head. *Did she mean what I think she meant? Perhaps she meant "girlfriend" as in close female friend. She certainly didn't mean lesbian. Nah, she couldn't be one of "them." God, why do you get me into these kinds of situations?* I did my best to stay cool, and not let the "dialogue" be written all across my face.

Carolyn continued.

"Yeah, I study at a local hospital. My girlfriend's a nurse ..."

Oh gosh, I think Carolyn *is* a lesbian. Oh, she can't be, she's not manly acting, and she has long hair. Lesbians don't have long hair. Do they?

This conversation was not going as I had planned. I knew I had heard God correctly. I was convinced that He did want me to speak with Carolyn, but why?

But I decided that if Carolyn felt comfortable enough to use the word "girlfriend" so nonchalantly with a perfect stranger, I figured I could ask her about it. So without skipping a beat, I asked, "How long have you and your girlfriend been seeing each other?" I halfway expected her to flinch with an "Oh no, she's not my *girlfriend*, we're just friends" response.

"Two years," she said.

She *is* a lesbian. I wondered if now was a good time to pull out my Bible and just hold it and caress it gently.

As I sat there and listened to Carolyn share part of her story, she talked about her classes, her alma mater, and the possibility of buying her first home. The bubbly, cute graduate student in her mid-twenties didn't preach any *lesbian* gospel to me. She wasn't trying to proselytize her homosexual lifestyle onto me. She merely peppered her conversation with a few "girlfriend" stories. I didn't feel uncomfortable, violated, or strange, just informed about what was important to Carolyn.

Before long, our conversation was broken by the voice of the barista calling Carolyn's name; her drink was finally prepared. No more words were exchanged. We simply waved goodbye to each other.

Okay, God, I thought. *You've got some explaining to do. Why did I need to have that conversation? I didn't share any truth with Carolyn. She didn't walk away knowing what was important to me. Why did I have this conversation?*

All I know is this: I heard God speak; I listened to His voice and simply obeyed what He asked me to do. As confused as I was about the conversation, I knew God wanted me to have it. Sometimes you're not going to know the "why" of God's calling. The "why" is often irrelevant to the calling. We see this in

Scripture as well. For a long time, Abraham did not know why God had asked him to sacrifice his son, Isaac. David didn't know why he was chosen to be king. Daniel didn't know why he was held captive in Babylon. And Mary didn't know why God had chosen her to carry the Christ-child. Let's face it, to us, it doesn't make sense, but God always has a plan—and His plan is always perfect.

All of us need to pray for ears of missionaries. You may be reading this book right now, thinking, *Okay, what am I supposed to do?* If you're asking yourself that question; that's a great starting point. As I stated before, no one has mastered the missionary position. And in this case, practice does not make perfect; it makes natural. Just remember, no matter where you work, whether it is at Starbucks, McDonald's, *The Washington Post,* corporate America, the government, or anywhere else, it does not make a difference; your call to be a missionary is the same. Your environment is your mission field. Your personal faith story is your tool. Your God story is your message.

In the last chapter of this book, I'll share why I believe I had that conversation with Carolyn. You'll be surprised.

"All stories teach us something, and promise us some-thing, whether they're true or invented, legend or fact."
—Stewart O'Nan, modern novelist

COFFEEHOUSE GOSPEL TRUTH #2

HUMAN BEINGS DO NOT EVANGELIZE. GOD is the one who is in the business of evangelizing. His people are the witnesses of His truth. Do not be discouraged when your hard work seems to not be paying off. Remember, Jesus said no one can come to know Him unless the Father draws him. That's hard for all of us to understand. At least, it is for me.

The fingerprints of God are etched into the lives of all those who follow Him. Those fingerprints are very different in each of us. Some of us met Jesus while we were still in diapers. Our childhoods are filled to the brim with Bible camp, Sunday school, and church choir experiences. Others met Christ in the midst of feeling desperate and alone. Still others found the hope of Christ through tragedy and despair. I've even met people who have simply said, "Jesus dying on the cross for my sins made sense," and decided to follow Him. All of our God stories are different and creative and written by God Himself.

No matter what your story entails—mountain top highs, battles with depression, financial woes, sexual deviancy, beautiful childhood dreams, stardom, or poverty—the Gospel of Jesus makes your life story relevant and crucial to the retelling of God's story.

EIGHT HELPFUL HINTS WHEN YOU ARE TALKING GOSPEL

    1) Look the person in the eye.
    2) Smile—even when you're on the phone.

3) Wherever I go, I always try to carry a Bible with me. You never know when someone is going to need an encouraging word.
4) Be honest about your story. If you've screwed up in the past, don't be afraid to give the bad with the good. People respond to open honesty.
5) Don't force the Gospel on someone. Read their body language. If they're not interested, talk about the weather, Jennifer Garner, or politics. On second thought, stick with Jennifer Garner—politics is a rough topic, too.
6) Don't be afraid to admit there are aspects of Christianity you can't explain. No one can explain TBN.
7) Remember, becoming a Christian is more than just saying a thirty-second prayer; it's a realignment of all that makes up an individual. Don't shortchange the Gospel.
8) Avoid using the word "you." Instead, use "I," "me," "we," and "us." God's message is for all of us, not just the person you're talking to at one particular moment.

In Christian circles, we have long heard the term "testimony." I'm actually not a huge fan of the word. It just seems so dated to me, and I believe it's limiting, too. How many times have we each experienced an individual standing in front of the church body and sharing his or her salvation story? It's a joyous occasion to hear someone share the method God used to reach into their lives and show them love and mercy. I've often cried hearing the impact the grace and mercy of God has had on the lives of people.

However, when I use the word "story" in this book, it is not merely about your testimony; it's about the everyday life experiences all of us share.

Some may think the two concepts of a story and a testimony are interchangeable. I don't necessarily believe they are. When I think of one's testimony, I think of one's faith journey—a spiritual awakening, if you will. Your story encompasses much more than just your salvation narrative; it engulfs the entire picture of you. Your story is the good, bad, ugly, and precious parts of your life all wrapped up in one beautifully rugged package. No matter the contents or the wrapping job, Jesus wants to use our stories for His glory. We just have to be willing to let our stories be known.

Each of our life stories represents a statement. And each of us has the option to make lots of different statements with our lives. God uses these "statements" as testimonies to His faithfulness, mercy, and hope. Your personal connection to Christ speaks volumes, whether you think it does or not. It's uncanny how much one's "story" can light a path for a lonely traveler who is looking for a truthful home or simply a place to stay for an evening.

Sharing your faith in everyday conversations relies heavily on your comfort level in telling your story. Are you willing to open the pages of your story and read them out loud? Or do you tend to be the type who lets story opportunities pass without saying a word, thinking your personal story isn't good enough?

CONVERSATION #4 JANUARY 2003:
LISA MACK, COLLEGE STUDENT WITH A JEWISH BACKGROUND

I used to be a part of a leadership organization in my community that had a wide variety of members. Many of the members were from all over the world, worked very different jobs, and all had very different beliefs. Each year we would go on a retreat to a local national park and plan that season's events. Late night talks would inevitably occur, but no conversation was more engaging than one I had during my last term in the organization. I talked with Lisa about her Jewish faith and my belief in Christ.

"How do you believe you go to heaven?" she asked after we had been talking a while about our faith backgrounds, and then added, "You don't have to candy-coat it; I already know what you are going to say."

"Well, I believe that I need to put my hope and trust in the truth that Jesus is the Son of God and that He died on the cross to save us from the wrath of God. Because He died, we can go to heaven. However, not only must we believe that, we must believe in Him and seek to know Him in a personal way."

"So then what do you think about me? Do you think I am going to heaven?"

Uh-oh, I thought to myself. Obviously the answer was no, but how do I say it? Again she followed up by saying, "You can say what you think, I love having these talks."

"No, I don't," I admitted. "You see, the thing is, according to the Bible, none of us deserves to go to heaven. We only can get there through Jesus."

"Yeah, I can see how if that is what you believe that I wouldn't go."

I thought to myself, *God, I blew it. Should I have said something else?* Then He answered my question.

"Thank you, Matthew, for being so honest

with me. I have had so many Christians just tell me that I was wrong without wanting to hear about me and my faith. You didn't start with a conversion, you started with a conversation, which is all I wanted right now."

+Lisa continues to practice Judaism and teaches at the local synagogue. However, she did come to a Bible study I was leading to hear more about Jesus. We still talk occasionally.

A STORY ENGAGED

"Your cleansed and grateful life, not your words, will bear witness to what I have done" (Matthew 8:4b, The Message Bible).

In my last book, *The Christian Culture Survival Guide: The Misadventures of an Outsider on the Inside* (Relevant Books), I mentioned the impact author James Alexander Langteaux's message had on my life. In his book, *God.com*, James openly and honestly shares his life's joys, struggles, and questions in a way that is open and honest. As a result of this book, James' life story has influenced thousands.

James has told me he literally has received hundreds of emails from people all over the world who were moved and challenged to live grace-filled lives because of his willingness to be honest and candid about his personal story. James has told me many times how difficult it was to share openly. He questioned God on many occasions on whether or not he should bare his soul in written word. God said, "Do it." James listened and has been reaping the miraculous, life-changing stories ever since.

I am greatly aware of how fearful it is to be honest—especially in Christian culture. Christians are some of the most dishonest people on the planet. We often live our "in the world, not of the world" lifestyles like it's a T-shirt. When we walk outside into the real world, we wear our nicely fitted shirt for all the world to see, when many times the "T-shirt" is hiding the real us—the us that God can use to reach people. All of that ugly stuff we tend to cover up with fake smiles and happy words, God can use. You may not think so, but God can use anything for His glory if you allow Him to.

I don't believe we throw on our "T-shirts" necessarily because we're liars. But some of us are forced to live fake lives in front of our spiritual peers due to our fear of rejection, judgment, and ridicule. In so many instances, our fears win out, because the burden of judgment outweighs our desire and willingness to be open with others. This, too, is a battle to be selfless.

In April of 2002, while working at *CCM* magazine, I opened up in one of my editorials about my battle with anxiety and depression. I have long struggled with a mind battle of unhealthy thoughts and fear that caused me to begin taking medication for it about year and a half ago. In that editorial I wrote:

"The movie, *A Beautiful Mind,* has awakened many of us to the fragile aspects of the brain. As I watched John Forbes Nash (portrayed by Russell Crowe) endure an extreme mental battle between what is true and false in his reality, I couldn't help but see aspects of my own spiritual life. It's often very difficult for me to leave what I know is harmful thinking in the hands of my Savior ... I have to admit, I struggle with the concept of perfect peace. I want to experience peace, but it's a challenge for me to not be worried, depressed, anxious, or doubtful at times over very small or non-existent problems."

From writing those simple, honest words, I received countless letters from Christian music fans all over the United States who related to my battle with depression and anxiety. One of those individuals told me he had actually never heard a Christian talk openly about depression. He said he had left the Church, thinking his battle would not be understood. I felt so sad for him. I wrote him back and told him I have met countless Christians who have talked to me about their depression and anxiety. I also shared with him that he should not fear telling his pastor about his battle. God can use this individual's battle as a witness to His faithfulness and peace. But so many of us have a fear of talking about depression with other churchgoers. I believe the Church is supposed to be a hospital for the sick, lonely, depressed, and sinful—not a place where we shut down and live fake lives.

These types of struggles that all of us have experienced at one time or another certainly do help non-Christians relate to the Gospel message. It's my experience that much of society longs to relate to a common story. Commonality among life stories makes people feel like they belong—like they aren't a foreigner in world full of normal natives.

God's story of redemption through Jesus is indeed one large painting on canvas, and our life stories are the many colors from which the painter chooses to create His masterpiece. Every day, we have the capability to allow God to use our stories to mirror His. It's a matter of allowing Him to do so. You want to share your faith in everyday conversation? Are you an open book?

CONVERSATION #5 JUNE 2002:
JENNIFER COX, FOURTEEN-YEAR-OLD CHURCH KID

I met Jennifer at my church's senior high youth group. I was one of the volunteer leaders. She was fourteen at the time, and had the "reputation" of a young, skinny Monica Lewinski. The boys in my small group would refer to her as "head" queen. Yeah, that's a derogatory reference to exactly what you're thinking. You could tell just by looking at her that her mommy had made her come to youth group. From across the room, her demeanor seemed harsh and abrasive—exactly the kind of person I like to engage in conversation.

"What's up? You look upset," I said in my "I'm-trying-to-be-really-cool-in-front-of-the-high-school-kids" tone.

"Nothing," she said.

I'm thinking to myself, *Come on, little sister, you gotta do better than that to make me go away.*

"Nothing? You sure don't act like there's nothing wrong. You don't want to be here, do you?"

"Not really," Jennifer said.

"Did your parents make you come?"

"Yeah, pretty much."

"Yeah, my parents sometimes had to make me go to church, too."

She smiled at me. Ah, a connection.

+After that initial connection with Jennifer, she and I slowly became friends. Over the last couple of years, I've had the privilege of seeing

*her grow into a close relationship with Christ.
We eventually moved on from chitchat conversations to talking about deeper topics of
faith and life. When Jennifer graduates from
high school, she's decided to pursue social
work to help young girls cope with sexuality
and past mistakes.*

JESUS OPENED THE PAGES OF HIS STORY

Just today, in the midst of my insane, fast ap-
proaching deadline to finish this book, I had lunch
with the youth pastor of my church. While sitting at a
Jewish deli, my youth pastor friend asked me to take
over the church's junior high class for the summer.
Within the context of his question, he also asked me,
"How did you come about belonging to West End
Community Church?"

"Well, that's kind of a long story," I said, laughing.

Inside I was thinking, *I can't give him a five-word
answer. There has to be an explanation, a story, some
intrigue and substance to the answer I give.* I know;
I'm always a little dramatic.

So I shared part of my church story with him. I
didn't over explain; I simply shared enough of my
Christian background to give my answer some context.

Why did I go through so much trouble to answer a simple question? Because I wanted the five-word answer that I concluded my story with to make sense. I wanted Joe to understand my point of view. I wanted him to grasp that I didn't go about choosing West End Community Church nonchalantly. It was a calculated faith decision that took time.

When we share God's story, the logic is similar.

I can't tell you how many times Christians, not knowing that I am a follower, have approached me on the street only to babble off a quick fifteen-second Gospel presentation. As fast as their voices will move, and before I can stop them, they spout out, "Do you know if you died today whether or not you would spend eternity in heaven or hell? I can take you through some verses in the Bible right now, and you can leave here knowing that you'll spend eternity in heaven. Would you like to know more?"

Those I have encountered proselytizing on the streets aren't necessarily mean or invasive, just somewhat impersonal. They bear witness of God's apparent truth so fast that they sound like the last five seconds of one of those TV drug ads for Nexium or Paxil CR. You know the type—it's the commercial where for fifty-five seconds, we hear in glorious detail how wonderful Nexium heals our acid reflux; then we're mortified as the announcer completely changes his tone of voice and begins talking a thousand a words a minute. The commercial ends up scaring us with the thought that the "miracle" drug could cause headaches, diarrhea, stomach pains, weight gain, dry mouth, sexual side affects, or flu-like symptoms. It's not pretty.

No one wants to be force-fed Christianity. I've never met anyone who said they liked being forced to believe in Jesus. How many salvation testimonies have you heard in which a born-again person attributes the random street evangelist for his or her conversion? Probably not many.

Just look at the life Christ. He didn't give fifteen-second explanations about His own life; why should we downgrade the Gospel message with our sub-par Gospel presentations? Jesus took time to get to know people. He didn't hand out brochures to strangers telling them about His good works. He engulfed Himself into the world of humanity and told stories.

Most of Jesus' messages were delivered in the form of a narrative. He told stories so the average individual could comprehend His message. He knew that the best way for His message to spread was through His story. I believe that's why Jesus only preached a few times throughout His ministry, and instead opted for the story approach to bearing witness to His Father.

The disciples questioned Jesus about His constant use of stories in Matthew 13:10. "His disciples came and asked him, 'Why do you always tell stories when you talk to the people?'"

Jesus replied in Matthew 13:11b-13, "You have been permitted to understand the secrets of the Kingdom of Heaven, but others have not. To those who are open to my teaching, more understanding will be given, and they will have an abundance of knowledge. But to those who are not listening, even what they have will be taken away from them. **That is why I tell these stories**, because people see what I do, but they don't really see. They hear what I say, but they don't really hear, and they don't understand" (NLT).

Matthew 13 concludes with: "Jesus always used stories and illustrations like these when speaking to the crowds. In fact, he never spoke to them without using such parables" (NLT).

Even Jesus had days when His words did not penetrate the hearts of people. I find myself a little frustrated when I have spent time sharing my faith and nothing happens. But I had to learn quickly that my words will not always move people to bow to their knees and pray the prayer of confession. In fact, more often than not, they won't.

Gospel Truth: People will not always be moved every time you share your story.

When the message of Christ spread throughout the Holy Land, it was spread through story. When Jesus healed the sick, He was not only healing, He was giving people signs and wonders of His existence. People would leave Jesus and then would be seen whispering in synagogues about a miracle man—causing even more people to hear the story of Jesus. But not everyone believed, despite the fact that many of the stories were from those who had a first-hand account of Jesus' miracles and stories. But those who knew the truth didn't have to convince their friends and family to believe; they simply spoke out loud all that they had witnessed. They left the rest up to God.

That's exactly what I want my life to be—a constant expression of God's miraculous mercy. I want my actions and words to constantly display the work of my Heavenly Father. When I see Jesus heal the sick, I want to be one of those individuals who runs throughout the world sharing with others what I just witnessed. If we tell people our personal experience of God's faithfulness, we are bearing witness of all that God is. I can't force someone to understand; I leave that up to God. I just make sure I'm telling my stories.

Our stories make claim to all the attributes of God. They let people know what we have experienced through a life-changing relationship with Jesus. And just like some people responded to stories during Jesus' walk on earth, God will allow some to respond to Him through your stories.

INTERVIEW WITH HAMILTON SCOTT, FORMER CATHOLIC, NOW AGNOSTIC

Hamilton and I spoke about things of faith on several different occasions. He knew a little about my heart for God, but that's about it. He had a couple of very interesting encounters with Christians who were attempting to convert him. I asked him if I could interview him for this book; he said yes.

MT: Tell me about one of your experiences where a Christian shared his faith with you.
HS: A few years back, one of my good friends, Ryan, invited me to go along with him to one of his church parties ...

MT: Is your friend Ryan a Christian?
HS: Yeah, he is. He'd been a Christian for his entire life.

MT: Where was the party?
HS: It was at one of his church friends' houses. It was supposed to be a pool party.

MT: Ah, okay.
HS: It was funny because us guys weren't allowed to swim in the pool while there were

girls in it. It was really strange.

MT: Really? What denomination was your friend, Ryan?

HS: Freewill Baptist.

MT: Were you allowed to hang around the pool while the girls in the group swam?

HS: Oh yeah, we just weren't allowed to be in the water. One of the guys at the party told me that the "water" makes you do and think sexual things. There was a nine-year-old girl swimming in the pool alone, and we STILL weren't allowed to go in—and she was in there forever.

MT: What happened next?

HS: A couple of us guys were standing around, talking and eating junk food. One guy piped up and mentioned he was Jewish. Then, another guy at the party says, "That's great; my best friend is Jewish, too." The Jewish guy said, "Oh really, what's his name?"— and the Christian said, "Jesus Christ."

MT: Oh, gosh, I've actually heard stories about that line being used.

HS: Oh yeah, I was so mad. The whole party seemed like this big trick to get "non-Christians" in the same room as Christians. They even had a list where you sign up for more information about their church. The whole thing was tacky.

MT: Did you ever go to their church? (laughing)

HS: H---, no.

MT: How did this experience make you feel?

HS: I was pretty mad. I kinda felt like my time was violated. I felt like my friend had brought me to the party on false pretenses. I was there to have fun and get to know new people, but they were only interested in me being there if I was going to their church on Sunday.

MT: Have you ever had a good experience with a Christian talking about his or her faith?

HS: Yeah, I've talked to Christians who simply tell me what they believe, I tell them what I believe, and usually we both agree to disagree, but respect each other's differences. Mostly they're really good conversations, and not offensive at all.

MT: Thanks for your time, bro.

You ready to share your story?

"You may be insecure, inadequate, mistaken, or potbellied. Death, panic, depression, and disillusionment may be near you. But you are not just that. You are accepted."
—Brennan Manning, The Ragamuffin Gospel

A LARGE PART OF SHARING YOUR FAITH through everyday conversation is being able to relate to others in everyday circumstances. Like I shared in the last chapter, commonality in actions, thoughts, and ideals is a great avenue for communicating the message of Christ. People *want* to relate to you. People want nothing more than for you to relate to them. In most cases, all human beings desire to relate to others. The common thread that ties the two together doesn't have to be thick, unbreakable, or long, it just has to be there and available.

A few months back, I was on an airplane from Minneapolis to Orange County, California. I sat next to a sixtysomething lady who was reading a book called *The Gospel of Mary Magdalene.* I knew the book was not a Christian book; I had heard it debated on Christian radio several times. But since I knew a little about the book and its contents, I decided to use this as an opportunity to open up a conversation about faith. Somewhat surprisingly, she opened up. She told me a little more about what the book said, which ultimately led to a conversation about her entire faith journey. She had roots in Lutheran and Baptist churches, then decided she would go to a Nazarene church, then a Charismatic church, but recently ended up leaving the Christian faith altogether in pursuit of a self-taught religion that was basically a smorgasbord of Jewish, Hindu, Muslim, and Christian thought.

"I grew up in the Baptist church, too," I said.

"You did? Well, then you know what it's all about. I

hated church life. You know what I mean?"

"Yeah, I do. But what does your new faith think about Jesus?"

"I'm not really sure; I believe he was a good teacher, but certainly not the savior of mankind. Even as a kid in church, I thought the belief of Jesus dying on the cross for my sins was hogwash."

"Well, you and I differ a bit on that. I do believe Jesus is the Savior, but I can understand your frustration with church. But I have also witnessed God's power in my life. I'm not sure where I'd be if it weren't for Jesus."

"Hmm. Well, we'll have to agree to disagree, there. Tell me a little more about your childhood faith."

My new friend and I bonded over a pretty heavy faith conversation that lasted most of the three-and-a-half hour trip across the country all because she was able to relate with my own personal frustration with the Church. By the time we landed, I had talked her into reading C.S. Lewis' *Mere Christianity* and told her I would be praying for her.

Relating to people isn't difficult; it just takes practice, guts, and a little gumption.

EXERCISE

The following seven questions are here to help you know some of the areas of your life that can easily be related to others. These are basic likes and dislikes, emotional topics, and meaningless topics. No matter how random a topic, it's part of your story and can be used to engage a listener. Take a few moments to read the questions and answer them.

1) Tell me about your hobbies. Are you a craftsman? Do you like to scrapbook? Don't be shy; list everything you like to do, even if you don't get to do it very often.

_____

_____

_____

_____

_____

_____

_____

_____

_____

_____

2) What gets you excited? What makes your heart skip a beat? Is it your boyfriend or girlfriend? Your spouse? Job? Sports? History? Write down everything that moves you to the feeling of all-out joy.

_____

_____

_____

_____

_____

_____

_____

_____

_____

_____

_____

_____

_____

_____

_____

_____

3) Who are your favorite people? Perhaps it's your
mother or father who have influenced you the most.
Maybe you tend to be a big fan of Brad Pitt. No
matter who it is, dead or alive, write down the most
meaningful people in your life and why you respect,
love, or follow them.

_____

_____

_____

_____

_____

_____

_____

_____

_____

_____

_____

_____

_____

_____

_____

_____

_____

4) When was the last time you were moved to tears? Even if it was for a silly, immature reason, write it down.

_____

_____

_____

_____

_____

_____

_____

_____

_____

_____

5) Write down one of your life dreams. _____

_____

_____

_____

_____

_____

_____

_____

_____

_____

_____

6) List ten of your favorite books of all time and why you enjoyed them. If you're not a reader, list movies, video games, CDs, or websites you enjoy.

1._____

2._____

3._____

4._____

5. _____

6. _____

7. _____

8. _____

9. _____

10. _____

7) Write down your top five favorite topics to talk about. It may be as big as politics, religion, sports, or entertainment, or it could be five very specific topics, such as World War II, 1950s sitcoms, Michael Jordan, or Mormon theology. Make a list of whatever interests you.

1. _____

2. _____

3. _____

4. _____

5. _____

WHY THESE QUESTIONS?

You might think these are strange or petty questions. In some ways, they certainly may be. But it's been my experience that a conversation about eternal matters can come from just about any topic of conversation. My father has witnessed to strangers a number of times due to a common interest in hunting. My sister has used home schooling as a way to share her faith.

I don't have a great number of hobbies, but I have watched many strangers become instant friends over a conversation about fishing or antiquing. My fiancé Jessica is an avid scrapbooker. She has our entire dating relationship beautifully laid out within a twenty-pound scrapbook binder. She spends hours on this stuff. To be honest, it freaks me out a little bit, but she gets so much enjoyment from seeing our sweet faces framed inside a papered sailboat frame with a little "flat," 3-D sticker (hard to explain) of a boat attached to it; she makes it hard to not get excited right along with her.

Jessica meets so many people through the hobby of scrapbooking. Whether it's at a convention she's attended (yes, they actually do have scrapbook conventions), or teaching someone she's met a few of her scrap booking tricks, Jessica has experienced quite a few interesting conversations while creatively pasting some pictures to a blank twelve-inch by twelve-inch piece of black canvas. Hobbies often break down mental and emotional barriers. They create strong bonds between people that can often lead to a more in-depth conversation about your faith.

The ministry Fellowship of Christian Athletes reaches thousands of students each year due to building on an individual's love of sports. I've met so many people who count FCA as the reason they have a relationship with Christ. Why? Because of an individual investing a little bit of time to share "sports" with someone else.

You would be surprised to learn how many large ministries were born out of a common interest. However, you certainly do not have to build a world renown or even a community ministry to make something like this happen; it can be a one-on-one meeting or simply a small group of people interested in the same things.

When my grandmother was still living, she would visit the local nursing home two or three times a week. She'd play bingo, tell stories about the "good old days," or just listen to the needs of those around her. So many times, she would come home in tears of joy because she was able to share her faith with someone who didn't know Jesus.

COFFEEHOUSE GOSPEL TRUTH #4:

It is a major fumble to speak the Gospel in any way other than lovingly, mercifully, and graciously.

Each of those seven questions represents a different facet of our human personalities. There are many of these kinds of topics—certainly not limited to the seven questioned here. I call these types of topics "connectors." With well-executed transitions, we can learn to connect almost any part of our story to our faith in Christ—even if it's a simple topic such as Hollywood, hobbies, or dreams. You will be surprised to learn how many faith conversations can occur from some of the most random of topics.

It's kind of like the six degrees of Kevin Bacon. You've no doubt heard the theory that every actor in Hollywood has a "within six degree" movie connection with Bacon. It's quite possible this pop culture theory is flawless. I've never been able to break it. However, I believe, too, that our faith in Christ easily has six-degree connection with every topic of our story. Think about it. Name a topic of your life—even something as uncommonly talked about in Christian circles as bathroom habits, personal hygiene, and making love can be creatively turned toward the godly (not that you necessarily want to transition from talking about poop to talking about Jesus, but I've heard it done—only once).

Almost every topic can be transitioned back to God's story, and I'm not talking about "my best friend Jesus is a Jew, too" transitions either. Real, honest, natural transitions are very important.

For me, I can almost always turn a conversation about entertainment into a more meaningful talk about life. Because of my love and knowledge of music, movies, TV, and books, I find that simply having a varied list of favorites allows for a pretty extensive number of spiritual directions. Anytime someone asks me to list some of my favorite movies, I always include *Dead Man Walking* as one of the bunch. In my opinion, that movie represents the Christian faith unlike most of Hollywood's spiritual movies have done in the past. When I'm talking about books, anything by C.S. Lewis or G.K. Chesterton will do. I've even had a God conversation that originated from discussing FOX's TV show *The O.C.*

Jesus was the master of good transitions (His most famous transition, of course, was changing water into wine). But even when you don't include His first miracle, one can still see He constantly pursued turning basic everyday conversations or experiences into life-changing moments of truth.

Consider Jesus' conversation with the woman at well.

The Bible says in John 4, "Soon a Samaritan woman came to draw water, and Jesus said to her, 'Please give me a drink.' He was alone at the time because his disciples had gone into the village to buy some food. The woman was surprised, for Jews refuse to have anything to do with Samaritans. She said to Jesus, 'You are a Jew, and I am a Samaritan woman. Why are you asking me for a drink?' Jesus replied, 'If you only knew the gift God has for you and who I am, you would ask me, and I would give you living water.' 'But sir, you don't have a rope or a bucket,' she said, 'and this is a very deep well. Where would you get this living water? And besides, are you greater than our ancestor Jacob who gave us this well? How can you offer better water than he and his sons and his cattle enjoyed?' Jesus replied, 'People soon become thirsty again after drinking this water. But the water I give them takes away thirst altogether. It becomes a perpetual spring within them, giving them eternal life.'"

Though the woman came to the watering hole only expecting to draw a bucket of water to drink, Jesus used this opportunity to compare His truth to that of life-giving water.

You might be thinking, *But He was God in the flesh—of course His transitions were perfect!* Yes, you would be correct; the God factor certainly changes things a bit, but don't be so quick to underestimate the power of God in your own personal words. Your transitions may be bumpy and awkward, but you never know how God can use them.

If you're passionately pursuing the things of Jesus, His words are made alive in you.

WRITE DOWN YOUR STORY

Believe it or not, many followers of Christ have never taken the time to write their personal faith story down on paper. I think it's so very important to actually have your story in a tangible format. Some of you may not know where to begin; others could write six books' worth of information if they only had the time and energy. For those of you who have never written down your God story, here are few simple questions to help you get started. These questions are certainly not exhaustive, but they should spark enough thoughts about your personal faith story that you'll be able to have a clearer picture of how God has influenced your existence. It's my desire to see all of us use our narrative stories to better relate the message of Jesus to the world around us. But you have to know your story first.

If you're not a fan of writing, get a friend to ask you these questions and tape your interview.

1) What was your childhood like? Were you a churchgoer? Was a life in Jesus something you pursued? If not, did you believe in anything remotely spiritual?

2) When was the first time you remember hearing about God, Jesus, or the Christian faith? How old were you?

3) What was your immediate response to the Gospel?

4) If you grew up knowing Jesus, was there a time that you remember it really clicking? Can you explain this turn of events?

5) If you resisted your first hearing of the Gospel message, what was the main reason you didn't believe at first?

6) What ultimately changed your heart toward the Gospel message?

7) Were there any life occurrences—a death in the family, illness, a miracle, a new relationship, etc.—that stood out as landmarks to you on your journey of faith?

8) How did God use these life landmarks to pull you into a relationship with Him?

9) What attracted you to know more about Jesus? What part of your relationship with Him has influenced you the most?

10) What about your life changed after you made your decision to be a Jesus follower?

After answering these ten questions, ask yourself one more: *Is that your entire story?* Most likely, it's not. I'm sure most of us have pages upon pages of information, mercies, and narrative we could write about God's workings in our lives. Only use this chapter as a jumping off point. Use this as a place to begin. If you answered these questions thoroughly, you no doubt have a wealth of story to begin sharing with others. But don't stop here. It's important to keep coming back to your story and updating it on how God continues to influence your life.

CONVERSATION #7 MARCH 2004:
VARIOUS CHRISTIANS FROM AROUND THE COUNTRY

I asked several people the following question: *When was the last time you shared your faith with a complete stranger?* Here a few of the responses.

"Gosh, it's been forever since I talked about my faith with a stranger. I can't remember."

"Maybe a year ago? I think the last time was a conversation I had with my roommate in college. But that was definitely a while ago."

"I talk about my faith all the time. I think the last time was maybe a week ago on a Southwest flight to L.A."

"Every single day of my life. Sometimes even twice a day."

"Never. I am not comfortable talking about something so extremely personal—especially with a stranger."

"December 22, 2002. I remember the exact date, because it was the first ever meeting of my soon-to-be wife. I helped her find Jesus that day!"

WE ARE A SOCIETY BENT ON MAKING OUR voices be heard. From the politicians who boast their propaganda to entertainers who flamboyantly express their open-minded lifestyles to preachers who scream about a fiery hell, everyone seems to be saying an awful lot, but not listening—*really* listening—to what others are saying. Christians should be some of the best listeners, but sadly, in many cases, we're the worst.

I'm half embarrassed to admit this, but I'm an *American Idol* fan. I've watched it religiously since the very first season. I'm such a sucker for a good pop song and contagious stage presence. *Oh, the days of Kelly and Justin!* I have one pet peeve with the show. No one listens to Simon. I love Simon. I know he's somewhat mean and could be a little more tactful with his comments, but he's usually the only one with any advice, but people refuse to listen to him. They make fun and call him names, but don't listen.

I've always been told that one of the key ingredients to a great communicator is listening.

However, it seems to me that a foregone part of modern evangelism is the art of shutting up and listening. I don't mean to be harsh, but Christians have a tendency to be good talkers and very poor listeners.

Sharing your story through everyday conversation involves lots of sincere listening. If we want people to respect and understand our Jesus point of view, we must be willing to listen to the needs and thoughts of non-Christians. That's why it's important to be a good listener when sharing your God story.

Now I must be honest and say that I struggle in the listening department. If I have something "relevant" to say, by golly, I have the tendency do whatever is necessary to make sure I get to speak my mind. I sometimes talk without listening, and I know it's frustrating to others. In fact, it infuriates others.

Many times, for me, it comes back to my own selfish nature rearing its ugly head.

Most of the time—and I have learned this lesson the hard way—it is much more important to listen than it is to talk, especially when you're discussing your faith with others.

Have you ever had a teacher or an employer who seemed unable to hear you? It didn't matter what you said or how well you articulated it, they didn't hear you, because they didn't want to hear you.

A few years back, I had a boss just like this.

As the head of a large division of a Christian media company, Dave would listen to no one. He had the heart and mind of an intelligent and success-ful entrepreneur, but the people skills of a llama—a really stupid spit-in–your-face llama. No matter the conversation, Dave was always right; he was always the last one to talk, and it did not matter whom he was conversing with, he always got the last word. His employees—me included—were often left with the feeling that our opinions and thoughts didn't matter. Mostly we had these feelings because our opinions didn't matter to Dave. We were to be "yes" people.

Not giving others a chance to communicate their feelings, their heart, and their opinion is certainly a communicative taboo, but even more, it's an evan-gelical catastrophe.

Living in Nashville, I find it almost impossible to

visit a Starbucks without seeing other Christians having Bible studies together. Nashville doesn't have its nickname as the buckle of the Bible belt for nothing. Every time I walk into one of the many coffeehouses, there always seems to be someone witnessing or at least sharing his or her story. I *love* listening in on the way other people share the Gospel message. I know that's wrong, but I'm writing a book about evangelism, and I've been looking for some good content. (For those of you who have seen me listening in on your conversations, please forgive me.)

THREE TIPS ON THE ART OF LISTENING

1) Keep an open ear to what you hear a non-Christian say—even if it's a completely ridiculous statement. Remember, Nicodemus asked Jesus some really dumb questions.

2) Remember, hearing and listening are two very different objectives. You can often hear someone talking, yet still not be listening.

3) Jesus listened to the beggars and the prostitutes more often than He listened to the religious leaders. Come up with your own conclusion on this one.

One time in particular, I was sitting at a table, typing on my laptop, trying to listen in on a Christian man giving his spiritual spiel to one of the baristas who was on her lunch break. It was obviously the pair's second or third conversation about God, and the poor little barista seemed frustrated with her inability to respond or get a word in edgewise.

"The Bible IS the word of God, Cassie; it's your guidebook and your companion manual. Why can't you see that?" said the Christian man. "Did you read the book of Mark like I asked you to? If you want to understand who Jesus is, you need to work at it; you need to invest your time into trying to learn more." His was sounding more and more frustrating.

I could tell by her demeanor that Cassie was only half listening. Her face was blank. She seemed to be calculating in her head the remaining minutes until she needed to be back on the clock. The Christian man seemed to notice none of this. He wasn't listening to her; he kept talking and never allowing her to speak anymore than a "yeah" or "uh huh."

"You're so quick to discount the Gospel message. You go to your yoga classes; you take your college courses on Buddha, yet you won't take the time to try and understand Jesus. I'm going to pray that God gets a hold of your heart and mind, Cassie. I want you to believe. I don't want you to go to hell." (By this time, he was whispering his conversation for effect.)

"Well, I should probably be going," Cassie said. "My boss will be on my case soon."

And she left. The Christian man and I caught each others' glances. I just smiled and continued to type.

If we want people to hear us, we must hear them!

Jesus listened. He listened to Nicodemus. He listened to Mary Magdalene. He listened to the disciples. He listened to the beggars, the possessed, and the downright annoying. Heck, he even let Satan have His word. Jesus was an intense listener; He still is. He didn't pretend to be listening, only to be secretly thinking about how He was going to respond to those He spoke with; Jesus listened with the truth in mind.

We need to do the same.

CONVERSATION #8
BART DAMER, WASHINGTON D.C.

This story is from one of my good friends, Bart Damer. About four years ago, he started a small skateboard ministry in his church in Fairfax, Virginia. It began with a group of twenty skaters meeting on Sunday nights to just skate and hang out. It now has more than two hundred skaters coming each week. Bart has been able to share his personal faith with nearly every kid who has walked through the door. Many of those kids have a relationship with Christ now, because of Bart's personal love for skateboarding.

I'll never forget the day I received a phone call from my friend Greg, in California, letting me know that Pep Martinez had died at a club in New York City. Pep was a professional skateboarder from Washington D.C. who I had grown up idolizing. Back then, Philadelphia and Washington D.C. had taken the world of skateboarding by storm with names like Andy Stone, Stevie Williams, Chris Hall, Bam Margera, and many other guys who all ended up turning pro. I had always dreamed that God was going to bless my efforts to be a professional skateboarder so that I could try to impact the world of skateboarding for Christ.

Years went by. I blew out both of my knees (which God used to open my eyes and heart), and today I have the privilege of running a skateboard ministry at Fair Oaks Church, about fifteen miles outside of Washington D.C. Since the ministry started in 2000, God has allowed me to share my faith either directly or indirectly with local and professional skaters from all over the world! But most importantly,

God has allowed me to build relationships with many of the guys I grew up idolizing, including Andy Stone, Chris Hall, and ... Pep Martinez.

Shortly after I received "the call" from Greg, my cell phone rang again, and this time it was Andy Stone! (It's not every day you get a phone call from one of your childhood heroes.) Andy was helping Pep's family make plans for a memorial service at Freedom Plaza, the skate spot in D.C. that birthed all of these pro skaters. I used to head up there several times a week and skate. I'd always see Pep, Andy, and a bunch of the other locals skating there. Little did I know that ten years later, I would be asked to share my story at Pep's funeral.

Andy had urged the family to have me speak at the funeral. This was amazing to me, that an unbeliever (and someone I used to idol-ize growing up) was now contacting me to be the "religious" representative at the memorial service. The family was very hesitant to have anybody from any sort of religious organization participate. Yet Andy assured them that having me speak at the memorial was the right thing to do. To this day, it is still amazing to me that God worked through Andy to make sure that I had the opportunity to speak.

To be quite honest, I was terrified. I am not

a *"preacher."* While I get up and share my faith at Skate Night, the thought of a formal sermon scares me to death. As I began praying for this opportunity, I was filled with excitement, fear, doubt, hope, and faith that God would use me. Part of me wanted to get out of it 'cause I was so scared, but I knew that God had brought all of the events of my past together for this one particular moment. I would be speaking at the funeral of one of my favorite skateboarders ever. Who would be in attendance? How will this— generally speaking—liberal and atheistic crowd respond? You can't exactly stand up in front of Pep's family and friends and break it to them that Pep is probably burning in a hot hell right now, especially knowing they don't even really want me there.

It helped that I was able to talk about Pep and how much I admired his ability as a skateboarder. That really put the family at ease to know that I was not just a random preacher leading the ceremony ... I was a fan of their son. As I spoke from Ecclesiastes 7, it was intimi- dating to look out and see people I skated with in high school, as well as professional skaters who had flown in for the memorial. This was a sensitive moment in the lives of everyone in attendance. While some might see this as one *opportunity to preach hell, fire, and damnation upon all who do not believe ... I really did not think that was "What Jesus Would Do." Jesus is a comfort to those in need, a healer to the sick. I encouraged everyone to put their trust in Him, and He would be their provider.*

Afterward, I had no idea what to expect. I wondered if the "unbelievers" hated me for bringing "religion" into this situation. What would these pro skaters think? Would I be rejected by a group of people that had inspired my lifestyle and helped to define who I am? These thoughts couldn't help but run through my head.

Immediately after the memorial service concluded, Pep's family came up to me with tears in their eyes and let me know "how beautiful the words you spoke were." They actually told me that they didn't really want me there at first, but they were so thankful for the words I said. I was blown away and convicted at the same time for all of the doubts that had been running through my head. God continued to bless. Many of the skaters expressed a sincere appreciation for offering a message of hope. God had clearly worked through my insecurities. The mother of Chris Hall approached me and wanted to know more about my ministry at Skate Night.

She went on to encourage me and thank me for being a positive influence to the skateboarders. Chris, Andy, and several others thanked me for "doing what I do." Never in my wildest dreams would I have thought [back in high school] that one day God would provide the opportunity for me to be a spiritual role model to the guys I looked up to and admired.

LISTENING BEFORE THE CONVERSATION BEGINS

When Christians walk into an environment—any environment—our ears should be perked to the social, emotional, and spiritual temperature of the room. We should be asking ourselves questions like these: Who is here? Where are the needs? What is my responsibility? How can my story have an impact on the lives God has put in front of me today?

Listening to the "voice" of the room is important. I'm not talking about eavesdropping on everyone's conversations, although some of my stories may imply otherwise; I'm actually referring to being aware of your surroundings. Awareness is an important key to evangelizing.

Sound difficult? Don't be overwhelmed. It's not as hard as you might think. Remember, it's a mindset. Like any other discipline or action, it takes practice. I've learned to ask God to open my eyes and ears and emotions when I'm in the presence of others. It's sometimes scary how differently you see everyday situations. Instead of simply going about your business, you recognize the little things, like the woman in the corner reading a book by the Dali Lama or the teenager asking his father really hard "life" questions. It's awesome when God opens your eyes to the sudden needs of people all around you.

As discussed earlier, we need to remember there is urgency to God's call to share our faith. We never know when God will call on us to bear witness to His truth. In my own little world, He's constantly presenting me with opportunities to engage non-Christians. I know I miss some of those chances because I fail to listen to my surroundings.

There is an art to listening. It's an art that few people have mastered.

It's a sacrifice to allow someone else's words, ideals, and actions to take precedence over your own. But if you want your God story to be heard, it's a needed sacrifice. Your ability to listen to those you are sharing the Gospel with will only give them a greater respect for you and what you have to say.

THREE SIMPLE WAYS TO LISTEN TO YOUR SURROUNDINGS

1) Don't be afraid to ask people how they're

doing. You may get an honest answer, or you may simply get the normal, "Fine, how are you?" But either way, you've opened up an opportunity to chat.

2) Watch for ways to help people. It could be the simple acts of holding the door open for a mother and her two small children or letting an elderly person go in line before you. No matter how big or small the deed, that's not the concern; it's that you're listening.

3) Take the time to get to know the people who are helping you—servers, cashiers, librarians—whomever it is! You never know what may come about from the simple willingness to get to know some one new. Many times I have been able to share my faith with a server or customer service person.

CONVERSATION #9 APRIL 2003:
JAMES PINE, COLLEGE STUDENT

I spent some time doing a little college ministry in my hometown one spring. There I met a young man named James who was that type of individual who always seemed to be getting into trouble. I honestly didn't know if James was a Christian or not, but because of his troubled nature, we quickly got to know each other. I tend to connect with those individuals many dub unreachable. James and I developed a friendship in which he often would ask me my advice on life. Such was the case when he came trekking across campus one afternoon with his usual sly grin intact.

"Hey Matthew, can I chat with you for second?" asked James.

Knowing James, my first thought was, *Oh, gosh, what has he done this time?*

"Dude, I need to talk to you about something," James said hesitantly.

"Sure, man, what' up?"

"It's about sex."

"Okay. Cool. You're in luck; I like talking about sex." After a few laughs, we got serious.

"I just wanted to know if you think it is okay for me to have sex with my girlfriend?"

"Umm, okay. First, what do you think about it?"

"I'm not sure; I know my mom would hate it."

"Probably so," I said smiling, "but it doesn't matter what I think about it or what your mom thinks; it's really about what you and God think."

"I'm pretty sure God wouldn't like it, but I also think that sometimes the rules don't apply to everyone."

"Well, that's a nice thought, James, but if rules of sexual behavior don't apply to everyone, sounds like you've made you're decision to me."

"Yeah, but I don't know. I think that I am my own man. Sometimes mistakes happen, and that is part of being your own man. You know?"

"Dude, you don't need me to tell you what to do. Just remember that God is looking out for you and desiring for you to pursue Him. I know you were brought up in church, and I don't need to preach to you. I'm pretty sure you know the difference between right and wrong. Just let me know what you decide. Make sense?"

"So you don't think I should have sex with my girlfriend?" James said in jocular tone.

"Yeah, that's pretty much what I'm thinking. I'm praying for you, buddy."

+James came to me the next week and said he decided not to have sex. He still doesn't know exactly what he believes, but he does know who God is and often came to me during the two years we knew each other to ask questions about God, the Bible, and life.

ONE OF THE BIGGEST FLAWS I RECOGNIZE in today's evangelical culture is that so many people sharing their faith have an overwhelming lack of basic biblical and Christian knowledge on the topic of salvation. Going into spiritual conversations without preparation is stupid and a sub par method of sharing God's story. You certainly do not have to hold a doctorate in theology or be a minister or preacher, but knowing the basics of the Christian faith is important. I have had several young adults ask me my opinion about this question over the years, "What knowledge must you know before you can effectively share your faith?"

I've asked myself that question a thousand times. And I've heard an array of answers ranging from "just Jesus" to "memorize the core apologetics of the Christian faith and know how to defend them with biblical references." Sometimes when I'm sharing Christ with a stranger, I feel at ease, the experience is positive, and I feel like I can answer most of the questions asked. Other times, I'm completely out of my spiritual league. Even some atheists, who actually know a lot about Christian Scripture, get the better of me sometimes, and they say they don't believe in any higher power (which in reality, is a belief in something).

In today's culture, everyone from stay-at-home moms to fourteen-year-old "C" students to Harvard graduates seems to have opinions about matters of faith and spiritual security. Although much of the average person's thinking process is based on feeling or what they've been taught, I've found it to be quite difficult expressing Jesus in a relevant way to the various thought processes of non-Christians.

Of course, that's why your story is such an integral part of sharing your faith.

However, like we discussed in the first chapter of

this book, I believe part of our spiritual calling is to know the basic aspects of the Christian faith. Sure, our stories are an integral part, but they're not the whole. As we mature in our walks with God, we should certainly know more about the reasoning and factual characteristics of the Christian faith.

THE APOSTLE'S CREED

When it comes to the basics of Christianity, no other religious statement has been used more to state the core characteristics than the Apostle's Creed.

Some believe the Apostle's Creed finds its roots as early as the second century. Although some certainly argue the validity of this claim, that doesn't negate the fact that many Christians still use the Apostle's Creed today to state their basic belief system. Here's the modern statement as seen in many liturgical churches around the world.

I believe in God, the Father Almighty,
the Creator of heaven and earth,
and in Jesus Christ, His only Son, our Lord:

Who was conceived of the Holy Spirit,
born of the Virgin Mary,
suffered under Pontius Pilate,
was crucified, died, and was buried.
He descended into hell.

The third day He arose again from the dead.

He ascended into heaven
and sits at the right hand of God the Father Almighty,
whence He shall come to judge
the living and the dead.

I believe in the Holy Spirit, the holy catholic church,
the communion of saints,
the forgiveness of sins,
the resurrection of the body,
and life everlasting. Amen.

For anyone who desires to know and understand the basic principles of Christianity, I believe the Apostle's Creed is a good place to begin. Though it's certainly not a thorough coverage of our faith, and it does contain a few denominational references, this historic document is the most revered of its kind.

If you want to engage your community with the Gospel, it's imperative you know some of the basics of Christianity. Here's a quick rundown of topics mentioned in the Apostle's Creed that are extremely important to the evangelical experience:

IN THE KNOW #1

"I believe in God, the Father Almighty."

The first line states the obvious. "I believe in God" is of course a statement nearly 90 percent of Americans claim. Many would counter this claim by saying there is a huge difference between the God some of those 90 percent of people believe in and the God of Abraham, Isaac, Jacob, and Joseph. Theoretically, they would be correct. The gods of Muslim and Buddha are not the same as the Christian God.

The second part of the first line is even trickier. Christians engaged in their faith see God as a loving, gracious, just, and saving Father. In several instances, the Bible refers to God as Father—the most notably being in Christ's ideal prayer: "Our Father in heaven."

In his book, *Knowing God*, well-known author and theologian J.I. Packer wrote, "If you want to judge how well a person understands Christianity, find out how much he makes of the thought of being God's child, and having God as his Father. If this is not the thought that prompts and controls his worship and prayers and his whole outlook on life, it means that he does not understand Christianity very well at all."

Being able to articulate to others how you see God as a Father is pivotal to the Christian faith. God is a Father who protects. He works on our behalf. He sees us as His children.

Matthew 5:48

"Be perfect as your Heavenly Father is perfect." Christians seek to be like God the Father.

Ephesians. 1:17-18

"[I pray] that the God of our Lord Jesus Christ, the Father of glory, may give to you the spirit of wisdom and revelation ... that you may know what is the hope of His calling, what are the riches of the glory of His inheritance in the saints." God the Father provides.

John 14:2-3

"In My Father's house are many mansions; if it were not so, I would have told you. I go to prepare a place for you. And if I go and prepare a place for you, I will come again and receive you to myself." God the Father is preparing a place for us to be with Him.

IN THE KNOW #2

"[I believe in God] the Creator of heaven and earth."

"In the beginning God created the heaven and the earth" are the first words recorded in Scripture. God's supremacy over nature is written throughout Scripture, but the author dedicated his first chapter to the handiwork of God. The God of the universe designed everything we see around us—stars, trees, sea, fish, dirt, and blue sky. His creativity is seen in every detail of creation. God's creation reveals His grandeur, mercy, and power. But it also reveals the minute elements of His caring personality.

When sharing your faith with non-Christians, it's very important to remember that you're talking to one of God's creations. Every human being is created in the image of God—something He is very proud of and takes great delight in.

CONSIDER THESE VERSES OF SCRIPTURE:

Genesis 14:22
"But Abram said to the king of Sodom, 'I have raised my hand to the LORD, God Most High, Creator of heaven and earth, and have taken an oath.'"

Psalm 89:11
"The heavens are yours, and yours also the earth; you founded the world and all that is in it."

IN THE KNOW #3
"[I believe] in Jesus Christ, His only Son, our Lord."

Just in case you're REALLY new to this whole Christianity thing, the belief in Jesus as our Savior is the center of our faith. If you don't know this one, you probably shouldn't be sharing your story. Moving on to number four.

IN THE KNOW #4

"[I believe in Jesus] who was conceived of the Holy Spirit, born of the Virgin Mary, suffered under Pontius Pilate, was crucified, died, and was buried."

WHO IS JESUS?

That's the question today's culture is asking. Of course, if we could scientifically prove Jesus' strange and miraculous life, death, and resurrection, Christianity wouldn't be considered faith. It's by faith that we believe Jesus to be the Savior of the world.

The Jesus question has been posed on a grander scale due to Mel Gibson's *The Passion of the Christ*, books like *The Da Vinci Code*, and TV news specials on the life of Jesus by CBS and ABC. The person you're talking to about faith wants to know who Jesus is, too.

The fundamentals about the life, death, and resurrection of Jesus begin with His holy, non-sexual conception. Educators, theologians, and historians have debated Jesus' virgin birth for centuries. Jesus was not man and woman made—He was Holy Spirit conceived. This belief is crucial to the Christian faith. The fact that Jesus was conceived without the sperm of a man and the egg of a woman is the foundation of His blameless life. When the Holy Spirit put life into Mary's womb, is was a miraculous sign that this child was the coming perfect Messiah.

In section number four of the Apostle's Creed, we also declare Jesus' suffering under Pontius Pilate, His crucifixion, His death, and His burial. In order for us to explain the resurrection of Christ, we must be able to stress the importance of Jesus' death, first. The core truth of Christianity is found in Christ's death.

Just recently I was reading about a speech from David Brown, the author of *The Da Vinci Code*, in which he said he had recently discovered new and pertinent information about Jesus actually surviving the crucifixion. He intended to include this finding in his bestseller, but decided against it due to the facts not "holding water." Mr. Brown is just one of many, getting media attention, who works hard at researching and attempting to prove what Christians believe to be false.

When sharing our faith, we must be prepared to answer the hard questions that many non-Christians pose. It's important that we not only know what we believe, but can prove what we believe using Scripture.

I'm surprised how many people I encounter who

know the concept of Jesus' death on the cross, but don't know why God had to send His son to die for the sins of the world. The sacrificial death of Christ on the cross brought forgiveness for those who are repentant of their sins; it fulfilled the Old Testament law that required God's people to make yearly sacrificial offerings and paid the price of redemption once and for all.

CONSIDER THESE VERSES OF SCRIPTURE:

Romans 7:4

"So this is the point: The law no longer holds you in its power, because you died to its power when you died with Christ on the cross."

1 Corinthians 1:18

"I know very well how foolish the message of the cross sounds to those who are on the road to destruction. But we who are being saved recognize this message as the very power of God."

Hebrew 7:27

"He does not need to offer sacrifices every day like the other high priests. They did this for their own sins first and then for the sins of the people. But Jesus did this once for all when he sacrificed himself on the cross" *(NLT).*

IN THE KNOW #5

[I believe on] the third day He arose again from the dead.

Although the death of Jesus brings redemption to all who believe, Jesus' resurrection sets Christianity apart from any other religion. When He overcame death, He separated Himself from the gods of other religions. He displayed His might and worthiness. He proved, by conquering death, that there is life everlasting for those who follow after Him.

If Jesus had not resurrected, Christianity would be pointless. Without a living Jesus, Christianity, like Islam and Buddhism, would only be a good teaching or a select lifestyle, not a redeeming guarantee on one's life. You can't be a Christian and not believe in the power of God's resurrection of His Son, Jesus. It's too key to the overall concept of Christianity.

Who wants to worship a dead Jesus? Not me. And it would be a waste for anyone else to do it, too.

CONSIDER THESE VERSES OF SCRIPTURE:
1 Corinthians 15:13-14
"For if there is no resurrection of the dead, then Christ has not been raised either. And if Christ was not raised, then all our preaching is useless, and your trust in God is useless."

1 Peter 3:21-22

"And this is a picture of baptism, which now saves you by the power of Jesus Christ's resurrection. Baptism is not a removal of dirt from your body; it is an appeal to God from a clean conscience. Now Christ has gone to heaven. He is seated in the place of honor next to God, and all the angels and authorities and powers are bowing before him" (NLT).

John 11:17-26

"When Jesus arrived at Bethany, he was told that Lazarus had already been in his grave for four days. Bethany was only a few miles down the road from Jerusalem, and many of the people had come to pay their respects and console Martha and Mary on their loss. When Martha got word that Jesus was coming, she went to meet him. But Mary stayed at home. Martha said to Jesus, 'Lord, if you had been here, my brother would not have died. But even now I know that God will give you whatever you ask.' Jesus told her, 'Your brother will rise again.' 'Yes,' Martha said, 'when everyone else rises, on resurrection day.' Jesus told her, 'I am the resurrection and the life. Those who believe in me, even though they die like everyone else, will live again. They are given eternal life for believing

*in me and will never perish. Do you believe
this, Martha?'" (NLT).*

IN THE KNOW #6

"I believe in the Holy Spirit."

When Jesus prayed in the garden of Gethsemane,
He spoke of sending His followers the "Counselor"—
the Spirit of God—to lead, guide, convict, and protect
His followers. Jesus was referring to the Holy Spirit.
When you're talking about faith with an individual,
the Holy Spirit is no doubt one of the most important
aspects of the salvation experience. It's important for
us storytellers to be able to explain the Holy Spirit's
role in a Christian's life.

CONSIDER THESE VERSES OF SCRIPTURE WHEN TRYING TO CONVEY THE RESPONSIBILITY OF THE HOLY SPIRIT.

John 14:26
*"But when the Father sends the Counselor
as my representative—and by the Counselor
I mean the Holy Spirit—he will teach you
everything and will remind you of everything
I myself have told you" (NLT).*

John 14:17
*"He is the Holy Spirit, who leads into all
truth. The world at large cannot receive him,
because it isn't looking for him and doesn't*

recognize him. But you do, because he lives
with you now and later will be in you" (NLT).

Romans 8:3b-6

"God destroyed sin's control over us by
giving his Son as a sacrifice for our sins. He
did this so that the requirement of the law
would be fully accomplished for us who no
longer follow our sinful nature but instead
follow the Spirit. Those who are dominated
by the sinful nature think about sinful things,
but those who are controlled by the Holy
Spirit think about things that please the Spir-
it. If your sinful nature controls your mind,
there is death. But if the Holy Spirit controls
your mind, there is life and peace."

Romans 8: 26-28

"And the Holy Spirit helps us in our
distress. For we don't even know what we
should pray for, nor how we should pray. But
the Holy Spirit prays for us with groanings
that cannot be expressed in words. And the
Father who knows all hearts knows what the
Spirit is saying, for the Spirit pleads for us
believers in harmony with God's own will.
And we know that God causes everything to
work together for the good of those who love
God and are called according to his purpose
for them" (NLT).

IN THE KNOW #7

"[I believe in] the forgiveness of sins, the resurrection of the body, and life everlasting."

These final three topics are blatant benefits to following Jesus. Each one builds on, and is interrelated with, the other. Because of our forgiveness of sins through Jesus' blood, our bodies will be resurrected, and we will live forever in His kingdom. That's the promise of God.

A few thoughts to consider: If there is *forgiveness* of sins, there must be sin. Our sinful nature makes us aware that we are in need of a Savior. And all of us sin. Paul writes in Romans 3:23 that all men, women, and children have sinned and fallen short of God's glory.

JESUS SHARES A STORY ABOUT OUR SIN

"Two men went to the Temple to pray. One was a Pharisee, and the other was a dishonest tax collector. The proud Pharisee stood by himself and prayed this prayer: 'I thank you, God, that I am not a sinner like everyone else, especially like that tax collector over there! For I never cheat, I don't sin, I don't commit adultery, I fast twice a week, and I give you a tenth of my income.' But the tax collector stood at a distance and dared not even lift his eyes to heaven as he prayed. Instead, he beat his chest in sorrow, saying, 'O God, be merciful to me, for I am a sinner.' I tell you, this sinner, not the Pharisee, returned home justified before God. For the proud will be humbled, but the humble will be honored."

Christians believe in a second coming of Christ when those Christians who have died before us will be resurrected and our heavenly reign with Christ will begin. Consider Hebrews 9:27-28: "And just as it is destined that each person dies only once and after that comes judgment, so also Christ died only once as a sacrifice to take away the sins of many people. He will come again but not to deal with our sins again. This time he will bring salvation to all those who are eagerly waiting for him."

These seven "in the know" points only scratch the surface of all that Christians believe. But they do represent seven beliefs that are imperative to know and understand before truly being able to share your faith effectively and effortlessly. Knowing what you're talking about is a crucial aspect to being able to share your faith in the everyday.

CONVERSATION #9 MAY 2004:

I had the pleasure of interviewing a close preacher friend of mine about what he considers to be important to the act of witnessing. He agreed to let me use his comments in the book on the basis of anonymity.

In your opinion, what are the most crucial elements of the Gospel message that someone sharing their faith should know?

We are all sinners and hopelessly lost apart from Jesus. God loves us in spite of our sin and acted to redeem us.

Jesus was God's Son who lived in history and died as a sacrifice for our sin.

Real life is available to those who humble themselves, acknowledge their sin, and trust in Jesus' sacrifice rather than their own goodness.

Are there any key lessons that we can learn from Jesus' approach to sharing His message with others?

He loved people. He knew people. We need to do the same.

Once again, in your opinion, are there "bad" ways to evangelize?

Any method that fails to recognize the God-given value of any individual is less than God's best. Our methods must treat each recipient with respect and honor.

If you were giving an individual your best advice on how to witness more effectively, what would you tell him?

Listen. Learn to discover the person's story so you can speak in a way that's relevant. Each person has a perception of God and His will. How you approach each person should reflect how they see God.

THE ROMAN PATHWAY TO KNOWING THE MEANING OF SALVATION

A classic biblical approach to sharing the Gospel message is called the "Roman's Road." That's not my name for it, but one it has received over the years. I thought it would be good for you know the "pathway" of explaining salvation to a non-Christian using the book of Romans.

Romans 3:23
"For all have sinned and fall short of the glory of God."

Romans 6:23
"For the wages of sin is death, but the gift of God is eternal life in Christ Jesus our Lord."

Romans 5:8
"But God demonstrates his own love for us in this: While we were still sinners, Christ died for us."

Romans 10:9
"That if you confess with your mouth, 'Jesus

is Lord,' and believe in your heart that God raised him from the dead; you will be saved."

Romans 10:13
"For, 'Everyone who calls on the name of the Lord will be saved.'"

Romans 12:1-3
"Therefore, I urge you, brothers, in view of God's mercy, to offer your bodies as living sacrifices, holy and pleasing to God—this is your spiritual act of worship. Do not conform any longer to the pattern of this world, but be transformed by the renewing of your mind. Then you will be able to test and approve what God's will is—his good, pleasing and perfect will. For by the grace given me I say to every one of you: Do not think of yourself more highly than you ought, but rather think of yourself with sober judgment, in accordance with the measure of faith God has given you."

WHY ARE CHRISTIANS SO DARN STRANGE when it comes to evangelism? It's gotten to the point that it's embarrassing to let people know you're a follower of Jesus. And it's not because we're discomfited talking about our faith in Christ, either. Unfortunately, many non-Christians get images of "TBNesque"-type people in their heads when they hear you say that you're a Christian. It's a sad fact, but some Christians are just prone to leave a bad taste in peoples' mouths. Consequently, it's become difficult for one to be an avid God witness in today's culture. I have spent more than my fair share of time covering up the tracks of other Christians. I'm not sure about you, but I get tired of having to try to explain to my non-Christian friends why televangelists never stop asking for money or why Christians are so darn uptight or why we hand out Jesus tracks as if we're life insurance salesmen—"Here's the information, can I call you sometime next week to see if you're interested?"

Most non-Christians in society aren't so much afraid of hearing about your belief in God or even Jesus. It's that the tacky practices followers of Jesus use and have used in the past to share the Gospel have often turned off society to the "good news." And to be frank, I can't half blame them; I've been turned off, too. More times than I can count, I've had my own run-ins with Christians who attempt to evangelize to me using fear, pamphlets, hellfire and damnation, and other impersonal tactics. These kinds of situations leave me disenfranchised with my own faithful breed.

In September of 2003, I was rather uncomfortably donned in red, University of Wisconsin Badger gear (mostly because I'm a Duke Bluedevils fan). While walking the streets of Madison, Wisconsin, at ten in the morning, I was watching everyone in my hundred-yard radius drinking American beer—and lots of it. I was thinking to myself: *It's ten in the morning, people! Isn't a little too early to be intoxicated?* Apparently, it wasn't too early for these people; there were funnels, kegs, and half-naked, drunken college students everywhere I looked. It was quite an entertaining scene—better than any reality TV show I had ever seen.

My fiancée Jessica graduated from the University of Wisconsin, and before she would agree to marry me, she insisted that I experience an infamous Wisconsin Badgers football game and all the mayhem of festivities that went along with it. And even though the game wasn't going to begin for at least three more hours, by the looks of it, there was a lot of mayhem.

Jessica wanted me to meet a few of her friends, so we were walking up the football stadium's main drag to one of the few "Christian" houses on the grounds of the school proudly touted as "one of the most" liberal universities in the nation. It was a pretty liberal campus. I had already seen my share of people rallying for various causes—gay marriage, abortion, and Howard Dean. The latter of those three was quite an engaging experience, to say the least.

But to my surprise, I was completely astonished to find a bona fide Christian bubble among the sinful havoc that surrounded me. You could easily pick out the Christians in this crowd of Wisconsin heathens—

they were the ones who were sober, wearing Jesus-gear, and seemingly running for spiritual "cover."

When we arrived at the "spiritual cover"—a huge sorority-style house—I instantly noticed P.O.D.'s "Boom" blaring out of the speakers that were set up in the front yard, and a large keg of *root* beer sat proudly on the porch. A couple of girls baring FCA T-shirts welcomed me to the "F.L.O.C.K." House. They were very nice people—almost eerily so.

Looking at Jessica with an inquiring grin, she leaned in and whispered in my ear, "Females living out Christ's kingdom."

"WHAT?!?" I asked.

"F.L.O.C.K. stands for 'females living out Christ's kingdom,'" she whispered again, except this time she had her distinctive shut-the-heck-up-and-smile tone.

Is this their idea of living out Christ's kingdom? I thought. Even as a Jesus lover, I didn't want to be standing among the pretty, root beer-drinking *flock*, so I'm pretty sure the twenty thousand other people basking in the decadence of their own sin had no desire to be here.

I helplessly stood on the porch of the "F.L.O.C.K." house, sipping my cup of warm root beer and listening to a couple of Christian college students discuss how wonderful their morning quiet time had been. It was like I had entered a little "Jesus" safe zone. As I watched a scene of collegiate chaos surround the bubble, I couldn't help but think: *How do we reach these people? I'm pretty sure the combination of root beer and P.O.D. isn't going to do it.* To be honest, I left the house of Christ-like females a little perturbed—not with them—but with the entire concept of modern evangelism as a whole.

It's a Christ-follower's ultimate goal to reach out to those who do not know the loving-kindness of God. Yet in the *flock's* case, as well as so many other ministry organizations, fraternities, and churches, they expected people to come to the safety of their environment to learn about Christ or hang out with those who do know Him. Unfortunately, we Christians have become experts at creating clean and safe surroundings for *ourselves,* but in the process, some of us have lost the true ideals of the Great Commission. *"And He said to them, 'Go into all the world and preach the gospel to all creation'"* (Mark 16:15). The Bible doesn't say, "Let all the sinners come to our little world of traditional religion so we can preach the hell out of them." It would be kind of humorous if it did, though, don't you think?

AN IMPERSONAL INTRODUCTION TO A PERSONAL RELATIONSHIP

It seems to me that many Christians have taken the personal connection out of evangelism. Somehow, we need to get it back. Relational connection is how Jesus related to those He led, and it's what He stressed as endearingly important to His disciples. For too long, mass-appeal evangelism has been the popular method of reaching people. Instead of all of us pursuing life as that of missionaries, we look for the easy way out. We hand out Jesus tracks. We expect pastors to be the only ones preaching the Gospel message. We erect Jesus billboards and wear "His" apparel. We treat Jesus like He's a movie star (maybe He is in light of *The Passion of the Christ*'s success), but I don't believe He ever meant to be marketed like a celebrity.

One day, not too long ago, I was driving on a congested city highway. My windows were down. I was doing my best job of rocking out to the local top-forty station, when an obnoxiously colored billboard proclaiming "Jesus Is Lord! Is He YOUR Lord?" caught my eyes. The religious promotion boasted a large painting of Jesus complete with three-dimensional arms reaching outward. It seemed as though Jesus Himself wanted to pick me up and give me a hug. At the bottom of the billboard, the name of a church and a pastor were cleverly advertised. My first thought was: *Leave it to Christians to try to promote Jesus to people who are driving eighty miles per hour around a crowded four-lane beltway.*

To be honest, drive-by evangelizing has become

a little awkward for me to digest, but to be *really* honest, I've totally done it. When I was a kid, an adult bookstore sat right next to one of the shopping malls my family and I frequented. Even at the age of fourteen (I was quite sheltered), I had no idea what went on inside an "adult" bookstore, but I had been told many times by my church's youth pastor that they were sinful. Once in a while, my friends and I would drive by the parking lot of the local adult facility and yell at the people who were nervously walking through the door. We'd scream: "Sinner!" "God hates you!" "Pervert!" "Jesus saves." We actually thought we were serving God by proclaiming damnation over the overweight, middle-aged men who tried to inconspicuously partake in adult entertainment. Not surprisingly, no one ever came to know Jesus through our random drive-bys.

Impersonal evangelizing has long been a popular means to a righteous end. During the '60s, '70s, and '80s, I believe it worked sometimes (although I have never been a fan of it). People were more open to hearing a black-and-white-no-room-for-gray message that made them feel convicted and in need of God's forgiveness. Christian culture as a whole took on a separatist's mentality. But it wasn't merely evangelists who carried themselves this way. We wanted our church messengers to be fluent men of God with a savvy knack for spiritual sound bites we could later quote to our non-Christian friends in the supermarket. Much like the popular speech where President Reagan told Gorbachev to "make my day," preachers were also known for making gutsy, blanket statements that invigorated a crowd of followers, but their approach hardly created a conducive environment for anything relational to happen. An invitation to become a follower of Jesus is a personal and intimate message—not meant to be auctioned off nonchalantly or delivered by car salesmen-like men and women who couldn't care less what your name is or where you came from.

Unfortunately, some preachers have never received the memo stating that their "wow-them-with-my-loud-and-clever-words" kind of communication doesn't work anymore. In today's culture, people don't want to be preached at, people want to be related to. I'm not sure God ever meant for the Gospel of Jesus Christ to be yelled and screamed from behind pulpits. Yet preachers have been preaching loud and proud for centuries.

I honestly thought this style of preaching was on the way out—that church leaders were beginning to see the need for relational evangelism to replace old methods. However, I recently attended a large Christian music festival and witnessed a well-known evangelist scream at the top of his lungs the message of Jesus for a solid fifty-five minutes. I couldn't sit there and listen to it. I didn't feel convicted. I didn't feel guilty or enlightened. I felt violated. I don't talk to my enemies in the tone of voice this particular man of God was subjecting this crowd to—and he was supposedly preaching the Gospel. His loud, obnoxious voice is still ringing in my ears today. This kind of preaching is insulting to the intelligence of non-Christians. It gives the impression that we don't think they're capable of understanding or relating to truth without it being screamed boisterously by a middle-aged balding man with bad taste in clothes.

A friend of mind used to tell me she believed God could use anything to get people's attention. Despite the Bible never mentioning God's witty use of marketing skill, campaign slogans, and loud, audible judgments to wake up non-Christians, I actually do believe He can use anything He wants to open the minds of people to the truth. He's God; it's His show. He's the director, producer, *and* writer of our stories. However, sometimes it's unfortunate He has to work with such lousy actors like myself.

Our God story is relevant when we deliver it in a merciful and loving manner. We must constantly ask ourselves if we are shortchanging the Gospel in the manner we present it. Are we doing those we're telling about Jesus a disservice when we show up "on call," ready to share our faith in the everyday completely unprepared, or, worse yet, with our fists of judgment in fighting position? The answer is obvious; of course we are.

But you know, I have learned I can't worry about how everyone else is sharing the Gospel. It certainly upsets me when I hear someone make a mockery out of Jesus' message, but I'm not that person's conscience. If we begin picking apart everyone else's methods, that's a significant amount of time that we lose out on sharing God's story. I can only be concerned for how *I* am presenting the Gospel. I can only continue to keep reevaluating my approach to non-Christians—to be sure that I make God's message be known with love, respect, and honor. Using our personal stories to share our faith makes it very difficult to offend or come as across angry or judgmental.

TODAY'S CULTURE IS A CONFUSING MESS

I sat at a restaurant table with twenty other people—a mix of friends, acquaintances, and friends of acquaintances. I tried to eavesdrop on all of the different conversations going on around the table (you can now tell I'm just a bit nosy). A couple Christians were sitting at this table—one male and one female. One young man, wearing a "Recovering Conservative" T-shirt, was an outspoken atheist. Another man talked blatantly about being bisexual. The girl down at the end, across the table from me, was a quiet democrat—obviously uncomfortable by the presence of several Bush/Cheney-supporting Christians. The bisexual man was talking with a gay Catholic man about his golf game. The atheist was attempting to rally support for his candidate down at the other end of the table. The two Christians were talking about fashion—with each other, of course. And I'm sitting there collecting a nice little anecdote to explain a point for my book. We were all different people, coming together for a simple dinner. Everyone was talking. No two topics were alike. Our agendas were insanely different.

This scenario got me thinking: Sharing your faith in today's modern culture is no easy task. Don't get me wrong; throughout history people have had different ways of thinking, but today, no one fears vocalizing their differences. If you're gay, you're probably out. If you're a conservative, you're probably boasting an anti-liberal sticker on your car. If you're sexually active with multiple partners, you're probably talking about it. If you're a born again Christian, you're probably, well, trying to figure out the most politically correct way to express your love for Jesus without offending the sexually active, the gay man, and the ultra-conservative—all at the same time. While the rest of the world gives little care to how their opinions and morals fly in the face of those around them, Christians still find it difficult bringing up "salvation" without suffering from the fear of offending the multitudes.

On campuses, at jobs, and in airports around the world, there are people who think of themselves as philosophers. Today's savoir-faire thinkers openly discuss everything from sex to politics to personal hygiene and everything in between. Just watch Comedy Central for about fifteen minutes, and you'll hear at least one comedian make jokes about going to the bathroom, pleasuring oneself, and the female menstrual cycle. No topic is taboo—except Jesus Christ and Him crucified—unless it's something *derogatory* about Jesus Christ and Him crucified. Everything else is fair game.

If you're anything like me, the mockery of Christ in culture is sometimes infuriating to you. But instead of it pushing me to remain angry about the mockery of my faith, I've found it to be quite entertaining trying to relate my relationship with Christ to those who do mock God. I've spent my share of time being stuck in the middle of beer-guzzling, pot-smoking groups of former university fratsters that certainly proved my strengths and weaknesses in sharing my faith in today's culture. There have been times when facing the cultural pitfalls of my lost friends that my outspoken reliance upon the mercy and grace of Jesus has been quite tempted to retreat into hibernation. But other times, I'm able to engage any crowd of non-Christians with my story.

I refuse to claim there are secrets to sharing the Gospel in today's social climate. As you know, every circumstance is different. To try to give you a list of rules to follow would be frivolous. Instead, I challenge you to use your personal God story to infiltrate today's culture.

Those of you who are bearing witness to Christ on today's mainstream campuses know better than I do the daily climate you encounter. Your issues face you every day in classrooms, on bulletin boards, and in rallies around campus. It does no good to challenge the professor in front of his or her students. You'll only hurt yourself, disrespect authority, and fumble the message you carry. But don't be afraid to ask the professor out for a conversation over coffee. Let him speak. Ask him questions about why he believes what he believes. What life experiences has he endured to formulate his current opinions? Let him or her know you're interested in them as people and not simply as a grader. He will probably still disagree with you in the future, but will no doubt respect your ability to listen and to be challenged. Some of the students I have spoken with ask me why they should do this when they know it will not change the professor's outlook on life. I always tell them it's because it makes them better at what they do, and lets people know where they stand.

The same is true in any environment. Be an active participant in the move of God. I read the book *Experiencing God* by Henry Blackaby several years ago, and the one thing I most remember about that book's message was Henry's challenge for Christians to not sit around and wait for God to plop something ministry-oriented in their backyard. He wrote that we needed to go seek out where the Spirit of God is moving and just join in. I realize that today's cultural limits are boundless, but even though our culture screams its love of sin at the top of its lungs, the same boundless limits extended to them certainly allow Christians to be that much more open-minded and creative in their presentation of their stories.

Your community needs you, and they don't even know it. Local community theaters need your assistance. Go and volunteer to coach your town's soccer team. Join the PTA, MADD, and other worthy organizations with causes you believe in. Hang out in a place where you'll meet people—at a coffeehouse perhaps.

Christians spend far too much time arguing apologetics amongst themselves. I've done it; I know it's fun, but too much of any one thing is not good. I realize that iron sharpens iron, but eventually too much sharpening leads to no iron.

My Christian friends and I hang out at dance clubs, martini bars, junior high football games, and the gym. Sure, there are times when we stick to minding our own business, but more often than not, we always end up meeting someone who wants to get to know us—and the God we serve. We aren't cheesy with it. We're quick to let people know how we met each other—at the church. We talk about life being hard sometimes—breakups, death of friends, and sicknesses. But mostly we ask people lots of questions, so we can get to know what makes them tick.

It takes a bunch of loving, grace-filled Christians to share Jesus with a community. Though the spiritual obstacles may very well be intense, we rely on the power of God to give us strength to endure what comes our way. Jesus didn't promise the disciples that sharing faith would be simple or popular; He said to be prepared for just about anything. They were willing to lay their lives and reputation on the line to be Christ's advocate.

IT'S AN UNDERSTATEMENT TO CLAIM
that Jesus loves people. While He was on earth, every
one of His words and actions expressed His profound
desire to care for us, intervene on our behalf, and
save us from living pointless lives. Jesus walked into
situations with His eyes, ears, and heart opened to
the needs of souls around Him. He hurt for the lost.
He ached for those without an eternal perspective.
His heart broke for the spiritually blind. His entire

three-and-a-half-year earthly experience in ministry was spent seeking to save the lost.

What is our attitude toward those who don't pursue Christ? Do our hearts break over the thought that someone may spend eternity absent from God?

I've begun praying that God would allow me to feel a fraction of the pain He feels for those who resist Him. I prayed this prayer not because I'm a glutton for punishment; I've simply realized that sometimes I have found myself to be so cold toward non-Christians. Not that I'm mean to them, but I just simply don't feel the weight of the void in their lives. I so often go through my day without thinking one selfless thought about the eternal value of others. I believe hell to be real, and every day, you and I come in contact with so many people who are running from God's reach. Shouldn't we be compelled by this thought to do something? Shouldn't our hearts—like Christ's—ache for those who do not know what it means to follow Jesus?

Remember Carolyn, the lesbian I met at Starbucks? She taught me something about sharing my faith. When she told me her story, she doused her conversation with the fact that she was a lesbian. It wasn't extreme, just enough for me to really understand what she was passionate about, what made her tick. Shouldn't our ability to share our love for Jesus be the same? Natural? Poignant? Like breathing? So many times, our attempts to be evangelical seem calculated, stiff, and abnormal. It doesn't have to be that way.

This is where our story paves the way for faith sharing to be simple, natural, and seamless.

The key to talking about faith in everyday conversations is allowing God to speak through us—letting His love come through each word, facial expression, and gesture.

I am a speaker on Compassion International's roster. Whenever I talk in front an audience, I will often talk about poverty, the needs so many kids face every day, and how an individual can help a child by sponsoring them on a monthly basis through an organization like Compassion. Because of my involvement with Compassion, I visited Nicaragua in January 2004 and experienced firsthand the value of this organization. Like with any trip to a third world nation, I was appalled by what I encountered. My heart broke when I saw the faces of these poor, dirty, stinky, kids. I was literally boggled by the environment some of these kids have to endure on a daily, weekly, and yearly basis. So many of us on the trip left this experience in tears—our emotional weight was heavy with all that we had seen.

I walked away not only aching for these kids, but realizing that my heart should break even more for those who don't know Jesus. Sure, this seems basic, but the truth is, I don't think about this often enough.

Our hearts and minds should be so in tune with the heart of God that the first thing we think about when meeting a new person is their soul. A few years ago, I, along with several of my friends, was sitting in a restaurant being loud, obnoxious, and maybe a little disruptive. About halfway into our meal, I noticed an older gentlemen standing rather close to our table, acting a little nervous. Before long he turned to our table, looked me right in the eye, and asked me this question: "I'm sorry to interrupt you, my name is John Sexton, and I know you don't know me, but I was wondering if you guys knew Jesus?"

I looked up at him, tears beginning to gleam in my eyes, and said, "Yes, all of us have a relationship with Christ, but I thank you so much for having the courage to ask us."

"I just didn't want to miss an opportunity," the man replied.

What a gutsy move. He had no idea how we were going to respond. We could have been the type of people to have chewed him up and spit him out onto the floor. Yet that didn't matter. He moved out of his comfort zone and engaged us anyway. Even though I'm not necessarily a fan of his approach, I was a huge fan of his heart and his mindset.

That man was an individual not living for himself, but living with the souls of others in mind.

All of us must do the same. All of us must answer

the call of Christ to be active participants in His story and learn to share our faith daily through conversations.

>> **AFTERWORD**

I WORK EIGHT HOURS A DAY AS A BARISTA at Starbucks. Some of the customers who frequent my store consider me to be their bartender. They say to me, "Drew, I feel like I can tell you just about anything." I laugh. But to be honest, I want them to feel free to share whatever is on their minds with me. I once thought that when these types of conversations occurred, I needed to find some way to present a well-executed plan of salvation at the end of every exchange.

I see things differently now. The end goal of my

relationships (specifically with non-believers) is not to share the Roman's Road with them. The Gospel is not the end of anything. It is the beginning of everything. It is in the middle of all things. Therefore, I find that as I begin relationships, I am opening up the opportunity to share the Gospel. I find that as I am listening and merely dialoguing with people on a real and honest basis, I am sharing the Gospel. As I sit and simply listen, I am sharing the Gospel.

One of my favorite quotes is by St. Francis of Assisi. He said, "At all times share the Gospel and when necessary use words." I believe that to be true.

Through my many encounters at the Starbucks, I have worked at truly getting to know my customers. I have had some customers talk to me about their struggling relationships, some have shared the great events in their lives with me, and others have even asked me for my advice on how to heal a broken heart.

It certainly doesn't begin that way, though. It all starts with them coming through the front door. After a few times, I ask them their name and memorize their favorite drink. Over time, we start to talk about life. I find that people are very willing to talk about themselves. I have found that most people desire to be open and honest. It seems that more often than not, many of my customers are looking for something to believe in.

Through their simple stories, my customers begin

to share their life stories. Consequently, I find as I experience life in Christ, I am able to meet a person in their story and then share mine with them, creating a common ground. We are all on equal footing as humans, lost in our human condition. It is Christ who transcends this condition and creates joy even amidst it.

In the conversations I have with my new friends, I feel completely free to be myself-truly myself-to express my fears and my weakness, and to express my joy and my love for Christ. I believe the Gospel permeates all of our lives, every aspect. Every day, we are experiencing Christ and His Gospel, if we really do know Him.

Christians have a responsibility in the life of the Gospel . As Christians, our life is the Gospel. We are part of the redemptive plan of God, so why hide our lives, our stories, from the rest of the seeking world? When we realize our part in the very Gospel itself, we assimilate it more into our lives. It doesn't matter if we have made mistakes. It doesn't matter if we don't have all the answers. We have Jesus. We have two ears that were created perfectly for listening to other people's stories and the ability to identify with the lives of others so that we might share the Gospel more thoughtfully.

Drew Tilghman, June 2004

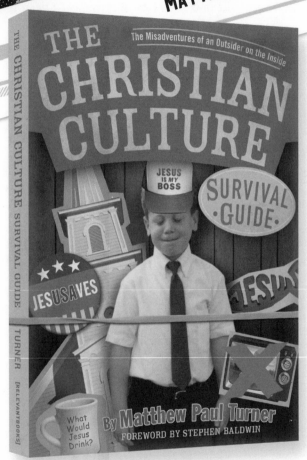